The Blanket Thief

Julie Oldfield

Grosvenor House
Publishing Limited

All rights reserved
Copyright © Julie Oldfield, 2025

The right of Julie Oldfield to be identified as the author of this
work has been asserted in accordance with Section 78
of the Copyright, Designs and Patents Act 1988

The book cover is copyright to Julie Oldfield

This book is published by
Grosvenor House Publishing Ltd
Link House
140 The Broadway, Tolworth, Surrey, KT6 7HT.
www.grosvenorhousepublishing.co.uk

This book is sold subject to the conditions that it shall not, by way of
trade or otherwise, be lent, resold, hired out or otherwise circulated
without the author's or publisher's prior consent in any form of
binding or cover other than that in which it is published and
without a similar condition including this condition being
imposed on the subsequent purchaser.

A CIP record for this book
is available from the British Library

ISBN 978-1-83615-057-2
eBook ISBN 978-1-83615-058-9

Dedication

To all animal rescuers everywhere. Saving one dog will not change the world, but surely for that one dog, the world will change forever.

Karen Davison.

Contents

Chapter 1	Orpington	1
Chapter 2	Cyprus	11
Chapter 3	Tammi	18
Chapter 4	Moving Mountains	24
Chapter 5	An Incredible Journey	38
Chapter 6	Reunited	47
Chapter 7	Disaster	54
Chapter 8	Brittany	63
Chapter 9	A Whole New Language	75
Chapter 10	Living with Tammi	84
Chapter 11	Devastation	91
Chapter 12	The Return	101
Chapter 13	Tammi's Legacy	109
Photos		114
Acknowledgements		125

1

Orpington

"You know what we need, Mark, don't you?"

"What's that, dear?" I noticed he didn't take his eyes off of the TV programme he was watching.

"We need a holiday. Just somewhere hot for a week, that's all. How about it, just you and me?" That's all it was meant to be, just a nice relaxing week in the sunshine.

"Oh, that sounds good, but I'm not sure I can get any time off at the moment; there's a big project coming up at work."

"There's always something going on; it's never a good time, is it? Maybe you just need to put your foot down for once and tell them you're going. Come on, we really need a break." I could feel myself getting upset, just thinking about the endless days ahead of us, with nothing to look forward to except work, work, and more work. As a community support officer for the Met Police, my job involved working some really unsociable hours, sometimes finishing at 2am. This meant having to get into my uniform and go to work when everyone else was coming home. I had started to resent not being able to spend time with my family; we were like ships passing in the night.

"What about going back to Cyprus? We had a great time there last year, didn't we? We can volunteer at the rescue centre again."

"Yeah, I suppose so, but what about the kids? We can't just leave them on their own. God knows what'll happen."

"Of course we can. They're old enough to look after themselves, and I'm sure they'll love having the house to themselves for a week. We can always get Rod and Chris to keep an eye on them. Come on, love, just think about it. We could be lying in the sun, drinking cocktails, beside that lovely pool in no time." Rod and Chris were good friends of ours from the church that we went to; our kids were the same ages and had grown up together. Marcus had just started university in London and was commuting by train each day, while Leah was still in her last year at school. They were great kids with lots of friends between them. We could definitely trust them to take care of the house and the dog while we went away.

"Alright, I'll see what I can do," Mark conceded. "But can we afford it? That bloody mortgage has gone up again; it's just relentless. I sometimes wonder why we bother working at all."

"What about your bonus? Isn't that due soon?" I smiled, hopefully.

"Yeah, let's just do it, Ju. We'll find a cheap deal and go for it. I'll talk to Geof tomorrow."

"Woo Hoo! Did you hear that, Kai? We're going on our holibobs." Mark laughed as I hugged our bewildered lurcher.

The very next day, I began searching for flights to Northern Cyprus. It was coming up to Easter, so they were quite expensive, but I wasn't going to be beaten; we really needed this holiday. I emailed the company that we had used on our last visit, hoping they would have another 'special offer' for us. One of the benefits of going to Northern Cyprus at this time was that it was still outside of the Euro zone, and things were relatively cheap compared to a lot of other places. We discovered this beautiful island by chance, really. A friend at work had been out there on holiday and came back raving about this amazing place. I decided to do a bit of research and uncovered lots of interesting facts about it, including why it was split into two separate islands. While we were there, we learnt a lot from talking to local residents and reading about the history of the island. In 1974, after years of hostilities, Turkish forces invaded Cyprus, and there was fierce fighting between the Greek Cypriots and the Turkish population. This led to thousands of people being displaced and the setting up of a United Nations buffer zone known as the green line. As Ercan Airport was built on land that officially still belongs to former Greek residents, it is seen as illegal to everyone apart from the Turks. The capital Nicosia is currently the only divided capital city in the world.

I received an email back from the travel company with the details of various packages they had on offer. The one that caught my eye included return flights and a week at the Pia Bella Hotel in Kyrenia. This was a fabulous place, where we had stayed on our previous visit. The kids loved the idea of having the house to themselves for a week, and I just hoped that nothing would happen to stop us from going. Once I had an idea in my head, I found it difficult to think about anything else. The sound of the phone ringing jolted me out of my daydream.

"Hiya." Mark sounded a bit despondent. "Bad news, I'm afraid, traffic's murder. I'm probably not going to be back until around eight. Just eat without me, and I'll have mine when I get home. Do you want me to pick Leah up from the gym?"

"Oh yes please, if you get back in time, that'll save me going out in the rain again."

Leah did gymnastics on three evenings a week at the Walnuts sports centre in Orpington while her brother Marcus was huddled up in his bedroom, playing computer games.

"Whereabouts are you? Is it the M25 again?" Mark worked for a large international brewery that had relocated from Kent to Bedfordshire. He loved his job, so decided to commute. This could sometimes mean a four-hour journey each way.

"Yep, looks like a car park. I've turned my engine off, as we're going nowhere at the moment. I'll let you know when I get across the bridge."

When the children were young, I often felt like a single parent, as Mark would have to leave early in the morning for work and not return until they were tucked up in bed. This endless round of work, kids and sleep sometimes left me depressed; I yearned for a different life, but I had no idea how I was going to change things. Despite working all the hours God sent, we never seemed to have much money to spare.

"Guess what? I found us a really good deal, and it means we can stay at the Pia Bella!"

"Oh, that's great. Geof's going to work out some dates for me tomorrow; looks like we're going on holiday!"

The weeks leading up to our holiday seemed to last forever, just an endless cycle of working, eating, and sleeping. But at least now we had something to look forward to. Finally, the big day arrived, suitcases were packed, cupboards were stocked with food for the children, and Kai, of course. We left strict instructions about locking the doors and windows when they went out and about. Also, various other useful information, like putting the bins out on Friday and feeding Kai twice a day. I tried not to think about all the things that could go wrong. I was sure they would cope; they were sensible kids.

One of the benefits of living where we did was our proximity to Gatwick airport. If the traffic was behaving, we could easily do it in around 40 minutes. I had to pinch myself in the car. Were we really going away for a week in the sunshine? Just the two of us. After checking our bags in and making it through security, we eagerly made our way to the food section. A nice, cooked breakfast was something we looked forward to before flying anywhere. We could never rely on getting anything edible on the plane; the vegetarian menu was usually very limited or non-existent. It wasn't long before our flight was called, and we made our way to the departure lounge. As we passed WH Smith's, I noticed a large display of Pen Farthing's new book, *One Dog at a Time*, in the window.

"Oooh, Mark, hang on. I've been waiting ages for that book to come out; it's about this amazing guy who rescues stray dogs in Afghanistan. I need something good to read on the plane."

"But you've already got two in your bag, and that doggy magazine, it's only a six-hour flight, love. Do you really need another book about dogs?"

I smiled as he shook his head and set off towards the exit, calling over his shoulder, "I'll go ahead and make sure they don't leave without you. Don't be too long."

I love to read animal books, especially true stories like this one. I don't think I've ever recovered from reading Anna Sewell's *Black Beauty* as a child. The mindless cruelty suffered by those poor horses still haunts me today. I snatched up a copy of the eagerly awaited book, noting the *Sunday Times* bestseller award splashed across the front cover. I couldn't wait to get started on this fascinating account of a Royal Marine who decided to do something about the stray dog population in and around Helmand province. As I waited patiently in the queue for the till, edging forward a millimetre at a time, I heard the final call for our flight to Cyprus.

"That's my flight. Can you hurry, please?" I asked the girl on the till, who looked utterly disinterested in me or my plight. She scanned the book and waited for me to fumble my debit card out of my purse. As soon as the till pinged its acceptance, I snatched the book out of her hand and legged it towards the departure gate.

Mark was pacing back and forth in front of the desk as I ran into the lounge, breathing heavily and struggling with my flight bag and newly acquired book.

"Blimey, Ju, talk about cutting it fine."

He presented both of our boarding passes to the flight attendant, and they ushered us through to join the end of the queue for the airport bus.

"Sorry," I gasped. "But look. How good is this?" I waved my latest treasure under his nose. "This guy's brilliant, I was reading about him in the paper last week; he's a soldier in Afghanistan, but he rescues dogs. It's an amazing story."

Mark grinned. "Well, I hope you brought a packet of tissues as well. I know what you're like when you start reading that type of book."

We were jolted forwards as the bus came to an abrupt halt, and people cried out as they were slammed together on the overcrowded vehicle.

"Looks like this is our stop." Mark pulled me closer to him as people jostled for space around us; everyone wanted to be first off the bus and onto the waiting aeroplane. We made our way painfully slowly up the steep, metal stairs, trying to avoid stepping on the heels of the elderly couple in front of us. Mark had our boarding passes ready when we finally entered the narrow doorway into the waiting aircraft. I began to feel nervous as we strapped ourselves in and settled down for the six-hour journey. Flying was not my favourite pastime, Mark thought it was brilliant, but I was just scared of dying.

I held on tightly to his arm as the huge engines roared into life, and we were propelled along the runway.

"Looks like we're off. Hold on tight." Mark smiled as he saw the terror on my face.

"It'll be alright, love, don't worry, hold my hand."

I dreaded the take-off and landing as I'd watched a programme which said that these were the most likely times that something could go wrong on a flight.

As usual, Mark fell asleep as soon as we got into the clouds, and I eagerly opened up my new book, inhaling that unmistakable heady aroma of paper and ink. I was immediately captivated by the amazing story of one man who decided to make a difference by rescuing stray dogs in a warzone. I am always in awe of people like him, those who just get on and do things, even when the odds are stacked against them. What drives them on? I wonder, when everyone else just walks away or tells them that they're crazy. My life is pretty ordinary, although my job requires me to intervene in difficult situations. I can't imagine myself doing anything extraordinary, I'm too much of a worrier. Mark snored his way through the drinks service, so I ordered him a beer and a large gin and tonic for myself. I thought I'd better wake him up for lunch, which turned out to be a rather disappointing salad sandwich.

"Enjoy your little nap, did you?"

"Just resting my eyes, you know me." He smiled. "How's the book?"

"Oh, it's great. You wouldn't believe what those poor dogs have to go through in Afghanistan. I'm so glad he's doing something about it; somebody should."

Mark nodded in agreement as he munched away on his sandwich. Several uncomfortable hours later, we landed in Istanbul, where a few passengers departed and several others joined us. Due to the political situation, there were no direct flights from London to Northern Cyprus. By the time we took off again, the plane was jam-packed with a menagerie of disgruntled people trying to squeeze themselves into the last available seats spread across the aircraft.

2

Cyprus

It was a relief to finally step out onto the warm tarmac at Ercan Airport. I embraced that lovely holiday feeling as we made our way on foot into the welcoming arrivals lounge. We retrieved our bulging suitcases from the loaded carousel and went in search of the coach that would ferry us to our hotel. A long line of similarly branded orange and green vehicles were lined up along the side of the road, just outside the terminal building. Eventually, we located a very stressed-looking driver waving a flimsy cardboard KYRENIA sign. As we tried to board the coach, people were also trying to get off. We moved out of the way to let them pass, only to be pushed aside by a large Turkish-looking man who seemed desperate to get past us.

"Oy! There's a queue here, mate." Mark stood his ground, and the man backed off.

It was the usual organised chaos that we had experienced before in Cyprus. We found a seat and settled down to wait for the boarding fiasco to run its course. It's funny how people arguing in a foreign language always sounds so dramatic! Cypriots are great communicators; they use their whole body to reinforce what they are trying to convey. Mark and I love a bit of people-watching, so this was a real treat. It was easy to spot the first-timers. The look of total bewilderment gave them away. We'd been there ourselves not too long ago.

Eventually, after many comings and goings, all the seats were filled, and we were ready to depart. We sped along the winding roads towards Kyrenia harbour, clutching the seat in front of us, as the driver narrowly avoided colliding with oncoming traffic.

"Bloody hell, he thinks he's Stirling Moss!" Mark exclaimed. My husband's not very good at being a passenger at the best of times; I kept hold of his arm to stop him jumping out of his seat. "Calm down! You know what they're like here. Just relax. We'll be there soon."

As we passed the local supermarket in Kyrenia, I noticed a couple of stray dogs waiting patiently outside.

"Look, Mark, I recognise those two dogs from last year. They look thin, don't they?"

"Probably because it's the beginning of the holiday season. Once the tourists start feeding them, they'll be OK."

There's a big problem with stray dogs and cats in Northern Cyprus. Many of them get run over as they struggle to survive in the ever-expanding holiday complexes. Poisoning of cats and dogs is common here; many Cypriots see them as vermin. Thankfully, there are a lot of ex-pats who do a sterling job feeding and caring for them.

It was dusk when we finally arrived at our favourite hotel, the Pia Bella. There were only about half a dozen of us left on the coach after several drop-off points along the route. Reclaiming our luggage from the cavernous hold took several minutes, as our driver had decided to wander off for a cigarette and leave us to it!

"Crikey, Ju, did you have to put so much in here? They weigh a ton."

Mark was sweating as he wrestled with the bulging cases; each one was filled with toys and treats for the dogs at the rescue centre,

"Oh, just a few treats for the dogs up at KAR." I smiled as he shook his head.

"Really, I think you've packed enough to feed all the dogs on the island!"

"Would you like me to help you, dear?" I made a half-hearted attempt to relieve him of my distended case.

"No, you're alright, I can manage. Thank God they're on wheels."

Dinner was always laid on for guests, whatever time they arrived at the hotel. On our first visit here we were very surprised when we were presented with a three-course meal at 2am! Dinner was delicious as usual, washed down with a few bottles of our favourite local beer. Mark let out a loud yawn as he checked the time on his watch.

"I can't believe how tired I am; it's only nine o'clock."

"I think you'll find it's closer to 11 o'clock here. They're two hours ahead of us." I pointed to the clock on the wall.

"Oh well, that's it then, I'm off to bed. You coming?"

"Definitely, I can't wait to read some more of my book."

We thanked the lovely waiters and headed upstairs to our first-floor bedroom at the front of the hotel. Our suitcases were parked in the centre of the room, where the porter had left them earlier.

"Let's just go to bed, Ju, we can unpack tomorrow." Mark launched himself on the bed and pretended to snore loudly while I struggled with the tiny combination lock, and eventually managed to get my nightie out, along with a toothbrush, of course.

In the morning, we woke up refreshed and eager to get downstairs and begin the day. Breakfast was cooked al fresco on the beautiful hotel patio, with the heat of the Cyprus morning sun streaming down on us. We were greeted warmly by several familiar members of staff and by some of the resident cats, who enjoy a happy life mingling among the hotel guests. One of the reasons that we particularly love this hotel is that in the afternoon, hundreds of the local strays are fed on leftovers and can be seen lining up eagerly outside the hotel kitchens. It's quite a spectacle, and many tourists come for afternoon tea on the terrace to witness this amazing sight.

We spotted Maria, the hotel manager, talking to some other new arrivals at the next table. Maria liked to welcome all her guests personally to the hotel. She looked across at us and made a beeline for our table.

"Hello, how are you two?" She beamed. "It's lovely to see you again."

"It's lovely to be here, thank you." We both smiled.

"I expect you will be visiting the dogs up in the mountains again soon?"

"Oh yes, definitely," I assured her. Maria had always taken a great interest in our visits to the sanctuary; she probably thought we were crazy, spending so much of our holiday there.

After a delicious, cooked breakfast, we hired a car from the hotel reception and made our way up the familiar mountain road to Kyrenia Animal Rescue Centre (KAR), nestled in the majestic Besparmak Mountains; this amazing place was just 20 minutes' drive from our hotel.

We were excited about seeing the animals and the wonderful people who take care of around 200 stray dogs and several cats there. The centre was opened in May 1999 on land donated by the Forestry Department. They have a fantastic, ongoing programme where they spay and neuter all the local strays before tagging them and returning them to where they were originally found. This helps to drastically reduce the enormous number of stray and unwanted animals on the streets of Kyrenia and surrounding villages.

"Oh, it's so nice to be back here, isn't it." Mark nodded in agreement, keeping his eyes firmly on the road in front of us.

"Look at all these new buildings going up. I don't remember seeing any of this last year."

Kyrenia is a popular holiday destination, and there is a lot of money to be made from tourism. Sadly, the infrastructure is not always available to support the sudden increase in construction, so many projects get left half-finished. Soon we were high up among the clouds as the road wound its way up the side of the mountain. It was amazing how quickly the landscape changed up here. "There it is!" I pointed to the familiar KAR sign perched on the side of the hill.

"Crikey, I almost missed it. They need a bigger sign."

Mark carefully negotiated the unmade bit of road that led down to the ramshackle collection of buildings which made up the rescue centre. We parked up and began to walk purposefully towards the familiar entrance. I stopped suddenly as something moved quickly in the bushes by the side of the gate. "Mark! Did you see that?" I whispered.

"What was it? It looked a bit like a fox to me."

"I'm not sure. Let's just wait a while and see if it comes back out."

We both crouched down and held our breath. After several minutes, a little black nose emerged slowly from behind the bush, followed immediately by the most beautiful pair of amber eyes, staring fearfully at us.

"I think it's a dog," I whispered. We stayed as still as we could, not wanting to frighten her. We could barely see her as she had buried herself deep inside the bush. We sat there quietly for a while, hardly daring to breathe. "She's beautiful," I whispered.

"What's she doing here?" Mark looked as confused as me.

"Probably dumped." He nodded in agreement. We had heard of several dogs and cats that had been cruelly discarded outside the rescue centre since it had opened. Sadly, not all the dogs survived due to the cold nights and the close proximity to the road.

We both stopped talking as there was the tiniest movement from inside the bush. A sharp snapping of twigs, then, very slowly, she crept towards us, sniffing the air excitedly. The little black nose twitched as she picked up the irresistible scent of sausages. Her beautiful, piercing eyes were full of fear as she fought the urge to run away. She quickly ate the little pile of sausages I had put down, stolen from the hotel breakfast bar. She froze, stared straight at us, just for a second, then she was gone.

3

Tammi

The old rusty gate at the entrance to the rescue centre was dragged open by Suzan, the centre manager. "Hello again, how lovely to see you back." She hugged us both enthusiastically.

"Oh, ouch! Sorry, I've got a terrible toothache." She unwrapped a thin, grey scarf and revealed a severely swollen jaw. I was shocked by her appearance; she must have been in agony.

"Have you been to the dentist, Suzan?"

"Yes, I've got some pills, but they're not helping. I've got the vet coming today, I'll get some painkillers off of him." She laughed. "Now come on in and say hello to everyone; there's lots of new residents. It seems like half the islanders are kicking their dogs out at the moment."

"Oh, look, Mark, there's Eddie." I made a beeline for the large, three-legged German Shepherd, who unfortunately had to spend his life on a chain, as he was not good with other dogs. Mark, meanwhile, was being accosted by a lovely, chubby ball of energy.

"Look, Ju, it's Grace, I can't believe she's still here." Grace was one of our favourites. She greeted everyone enthusiastically, with her permanently wagging tail, mugging unsuspecting visitors and relieving them of their treats. The place was overcrowded, as usual; there were several other chained dogs, and the group pens looked full to bursting. As we approached each wire cage, the dogs got excited, and the noise was deafening. All these poor little souls, just crying out for some human love and affection; it broke my heart to see them. The centre staff and the volunteers do a wonderful job, but the problem of discarded dogs and cats is reaching epidemic proportions in Cyprus. We were drawn, as usual, towards the puppy pens. I just can't resist puppy cuddles; they're always so pleased to have someone to smother with kisses. Just adorable. The sad thing is many of these little ones will never find loving homes, and the centre will be all they ever know.

Suzan was knee-deep in puppies, carefully lifting them one at a time to check them over. "Bloody people, I wish they would get their dogs spayed instead of dumping them outside." I knew this was one of her pet hates.

"Suzan, we noticed a little brown dog outside, hiding in the bush. Has it been dumped there?"

"Oh, that's Tammi. She's a bit of an escape artist, that little lady. Prefers to sleep outside, rather than in her pen. No one can get near her, apart from Yuliyan, of course. All the ladies love him." She smiled.

"Was she a street dog?"

"Yes, she was captured with another dog; he looked like her brother. They were both very skinny when they came to us. Unfortunately, he escaped from the van and disappeared before we could help him. I think she goes out looking for him, around the mountains at night.

"HELLO, hello, welcome back." It was the lovely Yuliyan, the only Cypriot keeper there; he was calling from inside one of the large pens. Surrounded by dogs, as usual, some hanging off his bright yellow wellies.

"How many dogs would you like to walk today?"

I was tempted to say, oh just one! But knew he would never believe me. Some visitors only take one or two at a time. We like to walk as many dogs as possible; it's so hard to leave any behind.

"How many are in there?" Mark enquired.

"Maybe seven or eight, I think, is good, yes?" He tried to count them, but they were all jumping around, eager to get his attention. It was an impossible task.

"We'll take them all, of course." I grinned.

There was a huge hullaballoo as the dogs were extracted one by one from their pen. The whole centre erupted with barking and howling as we made our way through the gate. It was a big relief to get out onto the dusty mountain path with our merry band of four- and three-legged friends. The sun was already hot on the back of our necks as we left the maelstrom behind.

The dogs are always beautifully behaved, and we unleashed them as soon as we got beyond the path.

"Look at them, Mark, they're just so happy to be outside. I love watching them, sniffing around, enjoying themselves."

They ran on ahead of us, eager to race each other up the mountainside. Just when we thought we had lost them, they would all come charging back, panting and slobbering all over us. Pointers are very popular in Cyprus, used as hunting dogs, then cruelly discarded at the end of the season. It was easy to spot these gorgeous dogs with their floppy ears and cropped tails. There are also lots of little, white, fluffy Cyprus poodles. Many are left behind when their families return home and don't want to pay for their time in quarantine.

We stopped halfway round and gave the dogs lots of treats and a drink of water. It can get extremely hot on the mountain, so it's best to go early in the morning before the scorching sun sets the dry, tinder landscape ablaze.

"Here, come on, fluffy, have some water,"

I set the little tin bowl down beside one of the more timid dogs. He eyed me carefully, then slowly stretched out his neck and drank thirstily. It always amazes me when dogs that have been so let down by humans are still willing to trust us. This had obviously been somebody's pet, probably bought as a cute puppy and then cruelly abandoned by his family. Life on the streets in Cyprus is no picnic, especially for vulnerable little dogs like these. Many are killed or injured by cars or motorbikes and left dead, or dying, on the side of the road. If they're lucky, someone will take them to the vets or bring them up to KAR. Surviving on the streets involves scavenging for food every day and avoiding people who are determined to do you harm. These dogs quickly discover places where they can hang out and are likely to get fed. They can be seen outside the supermarkets and hotels frequented by foreigners. Many of them are poisoned by hotel owners once the visitors return home. Without the rescue centre, a lot more of these dogs would die alone and in agony on the streets.

Mark sat staring into the distance, surrounded by a menagerie of wagging tails. He pointed down below us. "Look, we're actually above the clouds here."

"It's amazing! I know, so beautiful. These dogs are so lucky to have this place as their home. God knows where they would be without it."

It was peaceful up on the mountain; we sat there, lost in our own thoughts. It felt a million miles away from the hustle and bustle of Kyrenia town. Sadly, even here, the dogs were under threat, some had been victims of poisoning. There were people who didn't want them here, and they went to great lengths to try and eradicate them. On our last visit, someone had left some meat laced with poison along the mountain path. As the dogs came out for their daily walk with an unsuspecting volunteer, they hungrily grabbed the meat and swallowed it quickly. It became apparent that something was very wrong when the dogs started staggering around and frothing at the mouth. We were just setting off on our walk with a group of dogs when the distraught volunteer came back carrying one of the poisoned dogs. By this time there was nothing anyone could do except help collect the bodies. The sight of those poor dogs dying in agony right in front of us, on the side of the mountain, will live with me forever.

After a while, the dogs became restless; it was time to head back down. There was an old bath situated near the end of the walk. Several of the dogs relished the opportunity to jump gleefully into the cool water; they had a gay old time splashing around together. It's such a joy to see them all so happy and full of life, just like normal dogs.

We tramped slowly back to the centre with all the dogs in tow. Their tongues were hanging out as they sidled back up to the entrance gate. It was approaching midday, and the heat was scorching our shoulders. I was grateful that I didn't have to wear a fur coat!

Yuliyan was there waiting to return the dogs to their pen.

"Thank you, thank you." He smiled as he gathered up all the leads and gave each dog a quick cuddle before putting them back inside.

"It's our pleasure, really. We love it," I assured him. Although I was secretly looking forward to jumping into the lovely cold pool as soon as we got back to the hotel.

We visited the centre every morning on that holiday, armed with bags of leftover sausages and bacon from our hotel breakfast. I'm sure the waiters had their doubts about us being vegetarians! Each day, we would sit on the floor by the bushes outside the centre and try to coax Tammi out. Some of the other dogs came to 'help', which seemed to give her more confidence. She didn't like direct eye contact or sudden movements; anything like that would send her scurrying back into the bush. Gradually, she began to trust us and allowed me to stroke her; it took a bit longer for Mark, as she obviously had a huge fear of men. When we walked some of the other dogs, she would follow behind at a safe distance. We pretended not to notice as she scuttled along, moving stealthily from bush to bush.

By the end of the week, she had become quite used to us. I could hardly breathe as she allowed me to brush her thick, matted coat for the first time. I spent ages removing several ticks that had embedded themselves in her skin. These disgusting creatures bury their heads under the skin and gorge themselves on the dog's blood. I began by tentatively removing these with a special hook one by one; they made my skin crawl. It was important to remove the head intact, as these could cause problems if they remained buried in the dog's skin. The best part was splatting them on the concrete floor once removed. This was my introduction to the art of tick removal and other not-so-glamorous practices.

These days, I wouldn't bat an eyelid if I saw a tick on an animal. I sometimes look back and wonder who that girl was!

Tammi amazed us all by gradually accepting Mark, and she became quite attached to him. I think he must have made her feel safe. She began walking right behind him as we strolled around the mountains with our trusty little pack.

We had been sponsoring various dogs at KAR since our first visit in 2009. This time, we had been asked to choose a dog for one of Mark's work colleagues to sponsor. This was going to be a Help for Heroes sponsor dog; we had been given a special collar for the chosen dog to wear. The lady who had asked us had a son who was a soldier in Afghanistan. He had rescued a dog while out there, but the dog had sadly died. We took this responsibility very seriously, but how on earth could we choose one out of so many lovely dogs. In the end, of course, it was easy; it had to be Tammi. As it turned out, this became quite a big deal, and the local press got wind of it. Tammi proudly wore her collar, while the photographer struggled to get near enough to her to take a decent photo.

As always, the week flew by too quickly, and all too soon it was the day before we were due to leave. That final dog walk was so hard, and as we drove away, leaving our beautiful Tammi behind, my heart broke. Mark pulled the car over to the side of the road as

I sobbed my heart out. I had fallen in love with this little waif, and I just had to find a way to get her home. "What if she gets shot by the hunters? Or poisoned! We know she runs around the mountain at night; anything could happen. I can't bear to think of her all alone up here."

"I know, but it's so expensive. The cost of quarantine alone will add up to thousands of pounds."

It seemed hopeless, but something inside told me it was going to be alright.

"I don't know how, but I really think this is meant to be. We just need to trust that everything happens for a reason, and it's no accident that we're here now. Just promise me you'll help me to find a way to get her home."

"You know I will, Ju, but it's going to take a miracle to pull this off."

4

Moving Mountains

Boarding the plane home felt like I was abandoning one of my children. As we took off, I looked down at the disappearing landscape and imagined my poor little Tammi waiting under the bush for her daily sausage ration. She had trusted us, and we had let her down, just like everyone else. There were lots of tears on that flight and lots of silent prayers about keeping her safe until we could find a way to get her home.

"I just can't bear the thought of her sitting there, all alone."

Mark held my hand as I broke down again. "They will look after her, you know. She's spending more time inside the centre now."

"I know, but they've got so many dogs to care for, they won't have time to capture her again and again. Sooner or later, she's going to get killed."

Tears poured down my face as the plane took us further and further away from our darling girl.

We arrived in London at dusk, collected our baggage and made our way through the airport to collect the car. It was only a week ago that we had parked here and set off on our little holiday. It felt like a lifetime; so many things had happened in such a short time. I knew we had a big mountain to climb to get Tammi home with us. It was like a huge weight in my chest; I couldn't think about anything else. In my head, I was planning ways to raise money for Tammi's flight and to cover the huge cost of quarantine. Just thinking about her, stuck inside a kennel for six months, filled me with horror. She was used to living wild; she tolerated the semi-captivity of KAR, but to be locked up alone in a government facility might be too much for her.

It was lovely to get home and see the children and Kai, but I couldn't shake off this heavy feeling inside of me. We told them all about this amazing little dog we had found called Tammi. We had lots of pictures to show them, and they agreed that she was indeed beautiful. However, when we told them about our plans to bring her to the UK, they clearly thought we were mad. "How are you going to do that?" Marcus looked perplexed.

"I don't know, Marcus, but we just have to. We can't leave her there. She's just so vulnerable." I could hear myself saying these words, knowing how crazy I sounded.

"Surely the people at the rescue centre will look after her, won't they?" Leah's face mirrored my own as she picked up on my obvious anxiety.

"I'm sure they will, but she's such a nervous little girl, and she keeps escaping. She needs a home of her own, surrounded by love and care. I can't explain it, but I just know that she's meant to be here with us."

I was sitting on the lounge carpet, stroking Kai's head. He looked up at me with his trusting brown eyes. "You'd like a little sister from Cyprus, wouldn't you?"

We started fundraising straightaway. This involved organising raffles in our local pub and selling anything we could at boot fairs. It was hard going, as the amount of money we needed to raise was huge. Bearing in mind we had no savings, and our bank balance was usually overdrawn by the end of the month. It seemed like an impossible task. I was shocked by the cost of quarantine here in the UK; it could run into thousands of pounds over the mandatory six-month period. On top of that, there was the huge cost of transporting her here.

It was several months later, in September 2011, that we finally got our miracle. I can remember the exact moment like it was yesterday. When I was sitting at home watching the lunchtime news, my ears suddenly pricked up. I heard the newsreader say that from 1 January 2012, the quarantine laws were to be changed. Dogs entering the UK from inside Europe would no longer have to go into quarantine. There were certain requirements; they needed to have a passport, microchip, their rabies vaccination, and a follow-up blood test, along with internal parasite treatment, and a wait of three months before they were allowed to live in the UK. I was ecstatic; I couldn't breathe. For the first time,

I felt this was really going to happen. I got straight on the phone to Mark at work. "You won't believe what's just happened!"

I'm not sure he was best pleased as he was clearly in a meeting at the time. I wasn't deterred and relayed what I'd just heard on the news. "Are you sure it includes Cyprus? I'm not sure if they are officially recognised as part of Europe."

"Of course they are; they must be." I sounded a lot more confident than I felt inside.

"Ju, I've really got to go now, sorry I'm in a meeting with my boss. Just google it and make sure it includes Northern Cyprus. I'll see you later."

My hands were shaking as I typed the word 'Quarantine' into the Google search box. "Please, God, let it include Cyprus." My heart was in my mouth as several results came up on the screen. I began to work my way through them, carefully checking for exemptions.

The reason Northern Cyprus could be exempt was that, at this time, it was not an officially recognised country. The split between the north and the south after the war had left Northern Cyprus in limbo. Eventually, after several hours of searching different sources, I concluded that Northern Cyprus was probably included. I waited for Mark to get home from work, late as usual. "It includes Cyprus! I'm sure it does!" I accosted him with this news as he walked through the front door.

"Really? You're sure?" I led him into the lounge and showed him the information on the screen.

"You read it, I'm sure that's what it says."

He read it carefully in silence, then as he smiled at me, I knew. We had the confirmation that we needed. Our dream of bringing our precious Tammi home was finally becoming a reality.

Suzan from the rescue centre had kindly sent us a picture of Tammi looking very smart in her Help for Heroes collar, along with a copy of the newspaper story about her. I put the photo on the fridge door; it's still there today. Each time I looked at it, I promised her she would be coming home soon.

We had a bit of a reality check when we realised that in order to pay for her transport over here and her medical bills, we still needed to raise over £1,000. Mark was brilliant at fundraising, and he managed to gather lots of lovely things from his generous colleagues at work. We used these as raffle prizes in our local pub, The George and Dragon in Downe. We began to receive various sums of money from different sources; this was money we had no idea was due to us. The bank sent us a cheque for £500, apparently as a replacement for one we had failed to cash. To this day, I have no idea what this money was for, but I wasn't about to send it back!

I still look back in amazement at the way everything fell into place. I knew we were meant to save Tammi, and I had no doubt at all that it would happen. I do have a strong faith, and it's hard to explain what happened on the mountain that day. All I can say is I know we had help from somewhere.

We had spoken to Suzan, and she was delighted that we were going to adopt Tammi. She started the process of getting her micro-chipped and applied for a passport for her. She was taken to have her rabies jabs and wormed etc. By this time, she had been brought inside with some other dogs that were being prepared for their new lives in the UK. A lovely new kennel block with a corrugated iron roof had just been built; it was called Pine Walk. There was no chance of her escaping now; her days spent under the bush outside had thankfully come to an end. It would be terrible to lose our precious girl now, after everything we had been through.

We were keen to book a flight to bring her home as soon as possible. Turkish Airlines assured us that flying a dog from Northern Cyprus into the UK was not going to be a problem. They asked about the weight of the dog and the size of her travel crate. We were told to ring back with these details two weeks before our flight. It started to sink in that this was really happening, and we were very excited and a bit nervous about what we were about to do. I had spoken to various friends about adopting Tammi and had mixed reactions from them. Most people thought we were mad; some couldn't understand why we didn't just adopt one of the several thousand dogs in rescue centres here in the UK.

The simple answer is that we had fallen in love with Tammi, and we needed to have her home with us. The best way I found of explaining it to people was: imagine if you went abroad and fell in love, then someone said just go home and find a nice local boy or girl instead. Life just isn't that simple, is it?

So, there we were two weeks before we were due to fly out. Everything had been put in place, and Tammi was ready and waiting to start her new life here with us. We rang the airline just to confirm the weight and size of the crate, and disaster struck! They informed us that we couldn't bring her back on the plane as they did not have permission to carry livestock into the UK from Cyprus. We tried arguing with them about the previous conversation and the wrong advice we had been given. But it was no good. It transpired that DEFRA in the UK would not allow them to fly animals back here from Northern Cyprus. We asked for a refund, as obviously there was no point in us going if we couldn't bring her home with us. They refused. It still makes me mad now, just remembering how rude these people were at the time and how frustrating it was trying to deal with them. The worst part was when I rang back and pretended to be a new customer, booking the same sort of flight. They were still giving out the wrong advice. "Yes," they said, "it would be fine to bring a dog back from this area into the UK!" I was livid!

In the end, we decided to use the flight which we had paid a lot of money for. We needed to try to sort out some other way to get Tammi home.

I could barely bring myself to be civil to the flight attendants on the plane. I knew it wasn't their fault, but I was just so angry and sad that we would not be bringing our girl back with us. We landed at Ercan Airport late in the evening and made our way to the hotel. The staff were lovely as usual, but I just felt numb. Part of me couldn't wait to see Tammi again, but inside my heart was breaking. The next morning, we finished breakfast and made our way up the mountain road to the rescue centre. It was lovely seeing her again; she looked well. Amazingly, she seemed to recognise us straightaway. As we entered the kennel area, she crept around and avoided eye contact, but she couldn't help herself and gave it away with her happy, little tail wags. Yuliyan put her lead on and brought her out to us. "She's been waiting for you. Look how happy she is." We had learnt it was best to stroke her under the chin, as she got very nervous about having her head patted. As she stood there lapping up the attention, I felt really proud of her. She had come a long way, but we still had a huge mountain to climb.

It was shockingly cold in January. Having previously gone there in the spring or summer months, we weren't prepared for Cyprus in winter. It seemed such a waste to be staying at a beautiful hotel with two lovely pools when it was too cold to use them. We spent most of our time with Tammi, up at the centre. We wanted to get her used to going in our hire car. She was obviously very frightened of cars, and it took a lot of encouragement and sausages to get her inside one.

One day, we decided to take her to the local beach, which was just a short way down the mountain road. She was so nervous in the car that I sat in the back and tried to reassure her. We parked up and tried to get her out, but she was not at all keen. Then all at once, she shot out and tried to run away. Good job I had a firm hold of her lead, or heaven knows where she would have ended up. She was absolutely petrified. There was no alternative but to abort the mission to the beach and get her back inside the relative safety of the car straight away. As we waited calmly for her to summon up the courage to get back inside, the reality of what we were taking on began to dawn on us. She had been living semi-wild for a long time, and now we were going to change her life completely. She was going to have to face so many different challenges every day back in the UK.

"How on earth are we going to manage her?" Mark blurted out.

"We'll just have to." Hopefully, I sounded a lot more confident than I felt.

We had always had dogs at home, and I competed in agility competitions with our lurcher, Kai. Tammi, however, was a whole different ball game, but there was no going back now.

After discussions with Suzan and Margaret at KAR, it was decided that Tammi should travel over land with a group of about 14 other dogs, who were also going to the UK at the end of the month. Some of these were rescue dogs from the centre, who were going to their forever homes, and the others belonged to people returning home from Cyprus with their pets. This was a first for the organisation; they had not sent such a large number of dogs to the UK before. There was a lot of excitement about the proposed trip. The dogs were going to be travelling with a brilliant organisation called Animal Couriers. They are all lovely people, and they take great care of all the animals they transport around the world.

There was a lot of paperwork to do, and it all had to be in order for the various border controls along the way. It was going to be a long, arduous journey for all the dogs. For Tammi, this was going to be an extremely stressful time. Her deep fear of people and vehicles, along with the alien environment, would be difficult for her to cope with. There really was no other way, and we were so grateful for this opportunity; it just had to work. At this stage, we had no other option; we were just so desperate to get her home. Thankfully, we had just enough money left to be able to pay for her journey.

The end of the week came far too soon, and having to say goodbye to her again was soul-destroying. I tried in vain to hold back the tears after our final walk with her around the glorious Besparmak Mountains. Before handing her back to Yuliyan, I knelt down beside her and whispered carefully into her ear. "I'm so sorry you can't come with us this time, my darling girl. I promise it won't be long before you'll be home in England with us. You'll have to be very brave as you're going on a long journey. We'll be waiting for you, I love you."

She should have been coming home with us, but instead we had to stand and watch as she was carried back to her kennel. I couldn't bear to look at her little face as she watched us walk away again without her.

5

An Incredible Journey

The next few weeks were some of the longest of my life. The dogs were due to begin their journey in January, but due to the horrendous weather conditions in Cyprus, this had to be postponed until February. Several emails went back and forth to KAR over the next few weeks; we were so eager to get our little girl home with us it felt like torture.

We studied the weather reports for Cyprus every day; it wasn't looking good. There was snow on the mountains, and it seemed to get worse each time we looked. Our days were spent following the *Animal Courier's* blog on our old computer in the corner of the lounge. It was great to be able to send messages to some of the other owners and share our mixed emotions about the imminent journey.

Everything was ready for Tammi's arrival, including a comfy new bed. I wondered how a dog who had spent her life sleeping outside under the stars or on a concrete floor would adapt to some home comforts. Now it was becoming a reality, we were starting to get a bit nervous.

Mark stroked Kai's head. "What are we going to do if she doesn't like his nibs?"

"Well, she's not going back; we'll just have to cross that bridge when we come to it."

I tried not to dwell on thoughts like this. I can't deny they were there, usually late at night when everyone else was sleeping soundly. I sometimes woke up sweating as another nightmare scenario invaded my dreams.

There was a huge amount of paperwork to get ready before the dogs could leave for their new homes. We will be forever grateful to the people at KAR who meticulously sorted through all this red tape. This was a first for them too; nothing on this scale had been attempted before. If anything was not quite right, there was a strong possibility the dogs would be sent back to Cyprus. An even worse scenario was that they could be put in quarantine in any of the countries they would be passing through. We just couldn't bear to think about what this would mean for a dog as fearful as Tammi.

There were three couriers, one male and two females, who shared the driving and took care of five dogs each. They were driving a purpose-built, air-conditioned vehicle from the UK to collect the dogs in Kyrenia and bring them home. Their journey had started badly as they had encountered unprecedented levels of snow in France and Switzerland. This was not helped by the Greeks calling a general strike, which added another day to their already difficult journey.

"Mark, where's Igou-men-itsa?"

"Greece or Turkey, I think. Why?"

I sighed. "They've had to change their route again."

As someone who is geographically challenged, these places meant nothing to me. Luckily, Mark's time in the Navy gave him a much better understanding of where places are in the world. I just couldn't wait for them to arrive in Cyprus with the van that was going to bring Tammi home to us.

The couriers finally reached the port at Kyrenia, Northern Cyprus, three days later than expected. There was to be no rest for them yet, they had a boat to catch. Some of the staff from KAR had come down with the dogs and were lined up on the quayside to bid them bon voyage.

It was a tense moment as the customs officials inspected the courier's van. Everything had to be in order, or the group could have been delayed or prevented from travelling, something I find hard to comprehend, considering the general lack of animal welfare laws in Cyprus. It was exciting seeing pictures of them at the port in Kyrenia. Each dog had their name written boldly in black on a cut-off piece of green hose pipe, carefully threaded onto their collar. There was no chance of anyone mixing them up. We sat glued to the blog while all 15 dogs were carefully loaded aboard into their separate compartments. "Oh, look at her little face, Mark."

Tammi looked anxious as she was parted from her familiar keeper, Yuliyan, for the last time.

Far away in our lounge in Orpington, we sat squashed together in front of the computer screen, waiting for the update that would tell us they were on their way home.

"Is this really happening, Mark?"

As he smiled and nodded, I felt my eyes welling up again. I thought about the promise I had made to Tammi in Cyprus before we had to leave her behind.

Finally, we received the news we had been waiting for – It was all systems go. At last, after so many months of planning, they were on their way. For the first time, it seemed real; our little girl was coming home. I could breathe again.

Normal life went out of the window for us; every waking hour was spent following the blog and praying that everything would be fine.

"What's for tea, Mum?"

"Oh, sorry, Marcus, I didn't realise the time. Fancy a pizza?"

"We had pizza yesterday." Marcus grinned. "How about KFC?"

I tried to focus on other things, but the truth is, Tammi had captured a piece of my heart, and until she was here, I felt like part of me was missing.

Tammi's carer was 'M'. We now know him as Martin. At first, I was concerned that she would struggle to bond with him, knowing how nervous she was of strange men. But I needn't have worried, he was amazing with her and soon managed to gain her trust. He described how her tail would thump at the side of her compartment as she anticipated being taken out for a walk. All 15 dogs were walked three times a day, and on top of this, the couriers would spend time chatting to them and giving them lots of individual attention. Each day they used around 40 poo bags, 20 litres of water and a whole big bag of dog food!

After spending the night in a hotel in Tasucu, Turkey, the couriers had planned to take the shortest inland route to the port of Cesme. However, heavy snow had made conditions treacherous. They explained how they had discussed several different options over dinner and finally decided on a change of route. The idea was to drop down to the coast road and take the slower, snow-free route. Next day, they took the ferry across to the Greek island of Chios, where they finally entered the EU.

From here, it should have been plain sailing, as it was a route they had used previously without a hitch, but the Greek economic crisis had caused severe cutbacks in the government veterinary service. Critically, this included those authorised to clear paperwork for dogs arriving from outside the EU. It was also after 5pm on a Friday, which further complicated matters. The Greek civil service was working to rule – it would not open again until Monday morning. The couriers had no choice but to ensure the dogs were comfortable and secure while they found a hotel close to the port.

It was excruciating reading all these setbacks on the blog. It seemed like the whole world was conspiring against us. I sent the latest update to Mark, who was at work in Luton. I struggled to stay positive and spent the morning messaging some of the other prospective owners. Thanks to the daily updates on the blog, we'd got to know all of Tammi's travelling companions too: Bambi, Bo, Chester, Chief, Chloe, Choc, Freeway, Jack, Max and Paddy, Moira (aka Poppy), Mojo, Patch and Topaz. Some of them were already familiar to us, as we had walked them while volunteering at the rescue centre.

There were pictures every day of the dogs being walked in the snow by their dedicated carers, each precious little soul rescued and carefully prepared for a new life in the UK. Reading all the heartfelt messages left on the blog by the other owners each day was almost too much to bear. We were all full of hope that we would have our beloved dogs home very soon.

Monday morning, and after several cups of chai (this appears to be mandatory in Turkey), the couriers were able to pay their port tax and get on board the ferry. The next ferry crossing was from Gallipoli, on the Turkish border, known as Gelibolu in Turkish. I was reliably informed by Google that this is where the Allied forces landed in WW1 and suffered heavy casualties at the hands of the Turkish army. I learnt all sorts of things about faraway places throughout this time. I never dreamt that anything like this would happen to us; we were just a normal family, weren't we?

The spectacle of 15 dogs loaded into a single van was met with a certain degree of astonishment from the Turkish port officials. This was clearly not an everyday occurrence. Several more cups of chai later, and they were on their way to the Greek border. Here, they were asked to pay 20% of the nominal value of each dog; they estimated this at 50 euros! If only they had realised the true value of these dogs. To us, Tammi was priceless, and I'm sure all of the other prospective owners felt the same.

The last part of the journey took them up the long boot of Italy, past Rimini and Trento, through Innsbruck and from there straight through the tunnel to Calais.

As they made their way through Italy, we were treated to some beautiful pictures of the alpine scenery. Snow-capped mountains and stunning lakes surrounded the intrepid travellers. The couriers had to stop off at the vets in Perugia for the dogs to receive yet another dose of wormer. They crossed into France via the tunnel du Frejus. Here the amazed border officials eventually waved them through to continue the final stage of their journey. After a night spent in Lyon, their next stop would be Calais.

Sunday morning came, and the blog was full of beautiful pictures of snowdrops and yellow primroses.

Spring was coming early, ready to welcome our special cargo to Calais. This was a familiar place that Mark and I had driven through on several occasions, a landing platform to be quickly negotiated as we eagerly headed south at the start of another French holiday. Today, the images of the port captured our full attention.

A journey that should have taken 7 to 8 days had stretched into an epic 12 long days of agony for all of us waiting families. I knew deep down that the stress of this journey would have taken its toll on Tammi. She had been so brave for so long.

Amazingly, they sailed through French Pet Passport Control in record time. I've never been so happy about the sight of a P&O ferry leaving Calais. It must have been a huge relief for the couriers, too, as they could soon hand over their charges and go home to their loved ones.

Tears were streaming down my face as I turned to Mark. "They made it, they bloody made it!" We hugged and danced around the lounge, much to the amusement of our children.

Stunning pictures of the famous white cliffs of Dover filled the blog that had been such a lifeline to us. I swear, I saw those bluebirds flying over that day!

Once in Dover, two of the dogs, Max and Paddy, were whisked away by another courier to complete their journey, while the remaining 13 headed off to the collection point in Surrey. Some of the dogs had a bit longer to wait before they would finally meet their new families. A couple were heading up to Scotland, another was going to Manchester.

I was so desperate to see Tammi again I thought I would burst. "Oh, Mark, I just can't believe she's here in England. Let's get going. I can't wait to see her again."

Mark groaned. "But it's only going to take us about 40 minutes from here. They said not to come before two o'clock."

"There might be lots of traffic. You know what the M25 is like."

I stood by the front door with my coat on and a blanket for Tammi over my arm.

Mark grabbed his keys. "Alright, alright, let's go."

6

Reunited

"You have arrived at your destination." The familiar chequered flag appeared on the satnav's screen. "Is this the right place?" I struggled to make out the numbers on a row of similar-looking semis.

"Yes, it is. Look, the number's on the gate. I'll have to find a space to park down the road." Mark skilfully reversed into a tiny space at the end of the suburban street, and we got out of the car. I could feel myself welling up as we made our way towards the house. "She's really in there, isn't she?"

"Well, I bloody hope so." Mark grinned and put his arm around my shoulders.

"What if she doesn't remember us? I couldn't bear it."

Mark stopped and faced me. Tears were streaming down my face. "She will remember us, I promise. Now come on, let's go in."

"Hello, lovely to meet you at last, I'm Jane, one of the partners; you must be Tammi's mum and dad." We both nodded.

"Sorry we're a bit early, but someone couldn't wait any longer." Mark laughed. It was nice to be able to finally meet Jane; our only communication so far had been via a series of emails.

"Don't worry; some of the others have already been collected. You've all been waiting a long time for this. She's just in here."

We followed her through to the back of the house, into a small, dimly lit room.

"We haven't had a peep out of her; she's been asleep since she arrived. They were all exhausted, poor little mites..."

I was aware that Jane had carried on speaking, but my attention had been captured by an unmistakable silhouette, just visible in the far corner of the room. I felt the hairs on the back of my neck stand up; my heart was beating loudly in my ears. "It's her," I whispered to Mark. He nodded as I held on tightly to his hand.

At that precise moment, Tammi sat up slowly and stared straight at us with those gorgeous amber eyes. We were transfixed. At last, our beautiful girl was here; she looked dazed and a bit scared too. Tears streamed down my face as I edged slowly forward and instinctively crouched down on the floor, about six feet away from her. I'd been waiting for this moment for so long. I could barely breathe. I sat perfectly still, trying not to alarm her in any way. Then, very slowly, she crouched down low and crept towards me. Nobody said anything. She gently lay down beside me and placed her beautiful head in my lap.

There are no words to adequately describe how I felt in that moment. She looked so thin and vulnerable; the poor love was shattered. As I wiped the tears from my face, I was aware that Mark had shuffled up beside me. I looked at him for reassurance. "Is this really happening?" I whispered. "Can you pinch me, please? I think I'm dreaming," I had no doubt that there were going to be a lot of challenges ahead, but for now Tammi was safe, and we were all together again. I gently stroked her bony head. Her eyes were closed, but I knew she was listening to our whispered conversation. Every so often, her ears would twitch as if to say, I know you're talking about me.

I could have sat there forever. I just felt an enormous weight had been lifted off me.

The light was beginning to fade outside, and I knew we would have to be going soon. I carefully extracted my aching legs from underneath Tammi's sleeping head and stood up. "Thank you so much, Jane, I don't know what we would have done without your help."

She smiled as we both gave her a hug. "It's been a pleasure, honestly, to see all these lovely dogs go to their forever homes. It was touch and go in places, as you know, but this is the best part of my job. I hope everything works out for you; you've done an extraordinary thing."

Mark passed me the blanket we had brought with us, and I carefully wrapped it around Tammi's emaciated body. I was aware that she had lost a lot of weight since we last saw her in January. I handed her carefully to Mark, and we made our way outside into the street, and I got into the back seat of the car. "There's nothing of her, Ju; she's so thin." I nodded in agreement as he lowered her gently onto my lap. As we waved goodbye, I felt enormous gratitude for what the couriers had done for all of us. Thanks to organisations like this, run by genuine animal lovers, many more dogs and cats will be able to find their forever homes around the world.

Tammi settled down straightaway and appeared to sleep for the final leg of her journey. I gently stroked her head and whispered to her as Mark weaved his way through the evening traffic. Lights from oncoming vehicles would suddenly flash past, illuminating her slender outline before the darkness descended again.

"Do you think we did the right thing, Mark?"

"What do you mean? Of course we did."

"But look at her; she's like a bag of bones. That journey must have been hell for her."

"So, leaving her there to get shot by hunters or run over and left to die on the streets, like all the other poor bastards, would have been better?"

"No, of course not, I just wish we could have got her back quicker, that's all."

"Well, we can thank Turkish bloody Airlines for that, can't we?"

We drove in silence for a while, both lost in our own thoughts. Despite all the setbacks, she was finally here.

From now on, I was determined to give her the best of everything. There was nothing I could do to erase her traumatic past, but I could promise her a better future. She slept soundly across my lap while I told her how much she was loved by all of us.

As we got closer to home, my thoughts turned to Kai, our lurcher. He was also a rescue dog, removed from his previous owner by the RSPCA. He'd been found locked in a tiny cage with another puppy, both on the brink of starvation. A friend of mine helped with rehoming abandoned and abused dogs and knew that we had just lost our beautiful boxer, Alice. I didn't think I was ready for another dog so soon, but one look at that skinny little waif, with his sticky-out ribs and beautiful brown eyes and I was instantly smitten.

"Well, here we are." Mark eased the car into the narrow drive at the front of our house. Tammi sat up slowly, wondering why the gentle motion of the car had suddenly stopped. She backed away quickly as Mark opened the door and peered in at her.

"It's OK, lovely girl, you're home now. There's nothing to be frightened of." I tried to reassure her, but she wasn't eager to get out of the car.

"She'll be alright, love. I'll go and get Kai; he'll talk some sense into her."

Mark emerged a few minutes later with Kai, who was eager to see what all the fuss was about. He trotted over to where I had positioned myself beside the car, jumped up and gave me a quick once over before poking his long, slender nose in through the back door. Tammi watched him carefully and tentatively stood up and moved towards him. They gave each other a good sniffing, then Tammi jumped out into the garden. She was quite a bit smaller than him, and she allowed him to check her all over as she crouched down onto the grass. "I think we should take them for a little walk around the block, let them get acquainted?"

"OK, I'll go first with him, then hopefully she'll follow."

Tammi followed Kai out of the gate and along the footpath outside the front of our house. It was difficult to keep hold of her lead as she darted from one side of the pavement to the other. We lived on quite a busy road, and every time a car went past, she froze and threw herself on the ground. I could see that she was terrified. "Mark! This isn't working. She's scared of the cars. Let's go back; it's all too much for her." We turned around, and she immediately dragged me back to the safety of the garden. "I thought she was going to pull my arm off." I rubbed my painful wrist, where the rope slip lead had bitten into my skin. "She's quite strong for a little dog. Let's just get her inside, and hopefully she'll settle down."

This proved difficult as well. For some reason, she refused point-blank to go through the front door. We tried coaxing her in with sausages and bits of chicken, but she just would not budge. We had no idea how to handle this strange behaviour, so Mark just picked her up and carried her inside. I had made up a bed for her in the conservatory; it would be nice and quiet in there, away from the main living area. She ate her dinner as if it was her last meal and then sat down on the tiled floor, looking a bit bewildered. I bent down to stroke her, and she very gently put her paw into my hand. In that moment, I knew we had done the right thing. This was her forever home now, and we were going to take great care of our precious little angel. The children came to see her briefly; we didn't want to stress her out any more than necessary.

"Oh, she's so cute." Leah instinctively knew to crouch down low and give her some space. Both of our children had been brought up to respect animals. Horses and dogs had always been part of their lives.

"Kai seems to like her." Marcus laughed as Kai's long, pointed nose appeared from behind him. We knew we had to leave Tammi to settle down and sleep off all the stress and trauma she had been through to get here. It was difficult to tear ourselves away from her. Like new parents, we kept having sneaky peeks just to check she was OK.

We managed to put her lead on and coax her into the garden with Kai for toilet breaks, but she swiftly returned to the safety of her den. That evening, as we sat down at last, we were physically and emotionally drained. It had been such a long journey for us all.

7

Disaster

From the moment we brought Tammi home, normal life ceased to exist. Everything revolved around her; we wanted to make her happy in her surroundings as quickly as possible. Every tiny bit of progress she made filled us with joy. There were many firsts during those early days: the first time she crept into the kitchen, the first time she poked her head around the sitting room door, her first bark! Just small steps, but for Tammi they were huge. The environment was so alien to her; the inside of the house could have been on Mars, for all she knew. It became obvious that we had a huge amount of work to do; she was not like any dog we had ever known.

Things moved along slowly but surely during the next couple of weeks. Tammi continued to make steady progress. She crept around the house in what our son Marcus referred to as 'stealth mode'. As if she was waiting for someone to jump out and attack her.

One of her favourite pastimes was grabbing a blanket from the sofa, hiding it, and biting holes in it. She had probably never slept on a blanket before and didn't seem to understand what they were for. It's difficult to provide home comforts in kennels; blankets need constant washing and drying, which takes a lot of time. She often preferred to sleep on the cold, hard tiles in the conservatory rather than in her lovely, warm bed. Kai, on the other hand, was extremely attached to his home comforts. He was always snuggled up next to us on the sofa, burying his bony elbows into whatever crevice he could find.

We tried to deter visitors as much as possible during those early days. However, with two young adults in the house, this was easier said than done. When the children's friends came around, she would bark, then hide in the conservatory or behind the sofa. I lived in constant fear that she would escape because someone had left the front door open. I taped a large notice on the inside of the door, reminding everyone to keep it firmly closed. I thought that I had every escape route covered. I knew that we couldn't afford to become complacent.

We were still attempting to walk her with Kai at this stage. This was proving to be extremely difficult due to her being fearful of most things. Just getting out of the front gate took ages, especially if the local bus decided to go past at the same time. We were advised to use a slip lead on her, as these are difficult to escape from. However, every time she pulled back on the lead, it almost strangled her! After doing some research online, we decided to put her in a harness instead; this looked a lot more comfortable. On my days off, I spent ages just sitting in the front garden with her, coaxing her out of the bushes using chopped-up sausages. She was quite happy to sit there for hours with me and Kai, watching the world go by. I loved getting to know her and her funny little ways; she tried so hard to be brave. I just wished that I knew how to help her to cope with everyday life.

The long list of things that she found scary made no sense to anyone except Tammi herself. In her world, doorways were there to capture you and had to be avoided at all costs. This could have been related to the way she was brought into KAR, trapped in a cage, and ferried to the centre in a van. This had been done for her own good because stray dogs don't last very long on the streets of Cyprus. At the centre, she was kept in a large pen, which she escaped from whenever she could. What her life had been before she got to the centre is anybody's guess. Dogs are generally treated badly in Cyprus; many people see them as vermin, and poisoning is common practice. In Tammi's world, cars were big, noisy monsters. We lived on a busy road next to a popular local primary school. A nightmare for a dog like Tammi.

Sometimes, we did manage to get her out of the front door with a lot of coaxing and sausages. However, getting her to go beyond the garden gate proved extremely challenging.

"Come on, Tammi, it's alright, Kai's here to protect you." I thought my arm was coming out of the socket as

Kai made off up the road with me attached. Tammi, on the other hand, had decided to stay firmly in the garden. I wondered if we would ever be able to walk them together like normal dogs.

It became apparent early on that Tammi was absolutely terrified of traffic; she would cower and hide behind us whenever a car went past. Her eyes became wide and frantic, and she would even jump into people's gardens to get away from the scary monsters.

Men were a big problem for Tammi; she had begun to trust Mark, and it was fantastic to see her following him faithfully around the house. However, my twenty-year-old, six-foot-two son, Marcus, took a bit more getting used to. Every time he left his bedroom and went downstairs, she growled and barked, then quickly hid herself away behind the sofa. He tried desperately to avoid eye contact with her and let her know that he was a friend by throwing bits of sausage towards her. It was very frustrating for him, and I'm sure he wondered why on earth we had brought this crazy dog into our home.

Tammi gave Marcus's friends a hard time too. They often called round to play computer games and ended up getting involved in her rehabilitation. Most of them were brilliant with her and followed my seemingly ridiculous instructions diligently. No one gave her eye contact or encroached on her space, and they all knew to sit down quickly and ignore her unless she approached them. I had no idea at this stage whether we were helping Tammi or making her worse. There were lots of conflicting ideas about dog training on the TV and the internet. Not to mention all the 'helpful' advice given by unqualified friends and colleagues. It seemed everyone had an opinion on the subject, ranging from the Barbara Woodhouse brigade, who seemed to be obsessed with yanking the lead and commanding their dogs to 'SIT!' or 'HEEL!' every few seconds. To others who advocated for the use of electric collars and choke chains to ensure their dogs obeyed their commands. I instinctively knew that these methods wouldn't work with Tammi. She wasn't being naughty; she was just scared. The problem was, how could I convince her that she was safe now.

Sadly, my time at home with her was over too soon. For the next few months, I had to go on an intensive training course for work. I still got to see her in the evening, but Mark and the children got to spend lots more time with her than I could. I would leave home and catch the first train into London, then spend all day worrying about how she was coping at home.

It was during one of these training days that I got one of the worst calls of my life. Tammi was missing! She'd managed to get out of the garden and had disappeared without trace. Mark was beside himself. He had been out looking for ages before finally giving up and phoning me; he knew how devastated I would be. My class tutor could see by my face that something was horribly wrong at home and told me to go immediately.

The journey by train from Richmond to Orpington seemed to take hours, I was so desperate to get home and find my beloved girl. My mind was all over the place, imagining what could have happened to her; she was so vulnerable and terrified of everything. I was reliving every moment from the first time we saw her at KAR. Why did we bring her here only to lose her? What was I going to tell Suzan and Margaret? They had put so much time and effort into keeping her safe in Cyprus. How could we have allowed this to happen? We'd only had her for such a short time.

I was on the phone to Mark constantly throughout the journey. He'd been all over the local area with Leah, but there was no sign of her anywhere. There was nothing else I could do, so I posted her picture on all the local Facebook groups, hoping that someone might have seen her.

As soon as I got home, I threw my books down and grabbed Kai's lead. I knew we only had a small window of opportunity to find her before it got dark. "Come on, boy, we need to find your sister." Kai was just happy to go for a walk and happily trotted along beside me, oblivious to the sheer terror that I was feeling. Tears streamed down my face as I pleaded with God to keep her from being run over before I could get to her. I knocked on dozens of doors and accosted everyone we met, hoping that, just maybe, someone had seen her. I was getting messages of support on social media from all over the place, people asking whether we had found her yet. Friends in Cyprus and France, among other places, just willing her to be found quickly. Some people, however, were less than helpful. One particularly obnoxious man told me I should never have brought her over here in the first place. "Ah, that's the problem with those type of dogs, love. You can't trust 'em."

"Oh, really, well thanks for your advice, mate, I'll bear that in mind!" I pulled Kai away quickly before saying anything I might regret. I could feel myself sliding towards hysteria as I tried to hold it all together. Then, at last, a sighting in a nearby field, somewhere we had previously walked her. Mark rang me to say he thought he had seen her running across the field towards a busy main road. He couldn't run after her as he didn't want to chase her further towards the road, but now he had lost sight of her again.

I quickly made my way over to his location with Kai. I could tell by his face that he was as devastated as I was. "Where is she, Mark?"

"She was over there, in front of the trees." He waved his hand towards a line of saplings. "I called her, and she stopped and looked this way, but as I started to go towards her, she ran off again towards the road. I thought I'd better stay put; I didn't want to scare her."

"You did the right thing, but God knows where she is now. What are we going to do if she doesn't come back?"

"We'll find her, Ju, come on, don't give up now; we've come this far." He handed me a tissue, and as I wiped my eyes, I saw Kai looking up at me, probably wondering what had happened to his new girlfriend.

I patted his sleek, golden head. "It's alright, Kai, don't worry, we'll find her for you, I promise."

As the three of us walked around that huge field, calling Tammi's name over and over again, I began to feel completely desolate. This wasn't how it was supposed to end. Daylight was fading fast, and we both knew that very soon our precious girl would be all alone in the darkness. I couldn't bear to even think about her, scared and alone all over again. Why didn't we realise she could jump over a 6ft fence? She had escaped from the rescue centre so many times. We just naively assumed she would want to stay with us. "Oh God, where is she?"

Suddenly, we heard loud music playing, Mark's phone was going off in his pocket. It was Leah; she had returned to the house and was ringing to tell us that Tammi had just appeared in the front garden.

We ran the short distance home in record time. As we opened the front gate, there she was, just sitting there with Leah. Totally oblivious to the hell she had just put us through. Our beautiful girl, back in one piece. Exhausted, I sank to my knees onto the wet grass,

I wanted to hug them both, but I knew Tammi would be completely freaked out by it. Instead, I carefully held my upturned palm out towards her, and she slowly placed her paw into my hand. I couldn't speak as I had a large lump in my throat. Leah had tears in her eyes too.

"I was just coming back out to look for her, and there she was, just sitting there by the front door." Kai gave Tammi a good sniff and laid down beside her. I think he was pleased to have her back too. We knew we had been very lucky this time; many rescue dogs that go missing are never found alive.

"She was only in the back garden for a few minutes; when I looked round, she had gone. Scared the hell out of me. I didn't want to ring you, but I knew you'd kill me if anything happened to her." I could see the relief etched on Mark's face.

"She's back now; that's the main thing. We just need to be more careful in future."

I realised I sounded a lot more confident than I felt. How on earth were we going to keep her safe? We couldn't keep her locked away forever. Would she have been better off in her own environment? These doubts haunted me, especially in moments like this.

8

Brittany

By July 2012, five months after getting Tammi home, it became obvious that we needed some professional help. We were both exhausted at this point; coming home from work and having to deal with Tammi and her strange behaviour was putting a huge strain on our relationship. I knew that she needed more of my attention, and it was agony having to leave her each day to go to a job that I found increasingly frustrating. As a newly qualified police officer, I was drafted in to help with the London 2012 Olympics. This meant even longer shifts at work. In desperation, I decided to contact Elaine, who was a brilliant dog trainer, that we had stayed with before in Brittany. She encouraged us to come as soon as possible and stay in one of her gites, where she could assess Tammi and help us with her rehabilitation. We knew that the long car journey across France was going to be stressful for her, but two weeks in a quiet rural area, surrounded by nothing but open fields and woods, would do us all the world of good. At least we knew that her passport and rabies vaccinations were up to date.

By the middle of August, we were more than ready for our trip across the channel. As we were loading the car up the night before we were due to leave, I began to feel apprehensive. "We are doing the right thing, aren't we? It's going to be quite stressful for her." I looked at Mark for reassurance.

"She'll be fine, probably go to sleep just like Kai. We can't carry on like this, can we?"

"No, I know. I wish I knew what to do for the best. We just don't seem to be getting anywhere with her. She's so lovely; I just wish she wasn't so scared all the time."

"I know, I didn't think it would be so hard. Let's hope Elaine can sort her out."

"It's just so far away, after that horrendous journey she had coming here, now we're dragging her back across the channel." I could feel tears welling up in my eyes as the memories of her epic trip filled my mind.

"It's just France, Ju. Not the end of the earth! Six hours from the tunnel, and we're there. Do we really need all this stuff?" He shook his head as he piled more of Tammi's blankets into the back of the car. "We're only going for a fortnight."

"I want her to feel comfortable; you know she loves her blankets."

"Well, there won't be much room for wine on the way back."

I smiled because I knew exactly what was coming next.

"There's always room for wine."

We both laughed as he mimicked my favourite mantra. He closed the boot, and we walked back into the house together.

I don't think I slept a wink that night. I kept thinking about all the things that could possibly go wrong. We really needed this break; Tammi wasn't getting any easier, and I knew Elaine would be the one person who could help us. My stomach was still churning as the early morning light slipped through the gap in our faded, yellow bedroom curtains.

I got up and dressed quickly while Mark continued to snore loudly into his pillow. The dogs were still sleeping as I crept into the kitchen and put the kettle on. Immediately, two little noses appeared in the doorway, eager to see what I was up to. "Come on, you two, outside for a wee. We're off on an adventure today."

I smiled as they both trotted off happily into the garden. From the first moment they met, Kai had fallen head over heels in love with Tammi. He followed her everywhere, and when she became overwhelmed, he stayed beside her as if to say, It's alright, Tammi, I'm here. You're going to be OK. If only I could have made her understand that the long journey was going to be worth it. I was just about to take Mark's tea upstairs when he appeared in the kitchen doorway.

I looked across at Tammi, who had come back inside and was skulking under the table, trying to make herself invisible. "She knows something's up, look at her."

Mark shook his head wearily. "Well, we can't mess around with her today. She needs to get in the car quickly, or we'll be late."

Doing anything quickly with Tammi was a nightmare; she just got scared and panicked. "Come on, Tammi, let's get your harness on. We're going to find you some help, my love." I sounded a lot more confident than I felt.

She cowered down as I put the harness on her as carefully as I could. Seeing her like this made me want to cry. I spent countless hours trying to convince her that having her harness on was a good thing, but she didn't believe me. I couldn't bear to keep using the slip lead on her; it looked like a noose around her neck. I put Kai's collar on him and took both dogs outside, where Mark was struggling to fit the last of our luggage into the boot.

"Can you keep still for a minute? I'm going to try and get her in the car."

Tammi watched Kai jump effortlessly onto the backseat of our old silver Vauxhall Astra. I produced some cooked chicken from my pocket and tried to lure her in. "Come on, in you get, look what I've got, it's your favourite." She cowered down beside the car and looked up at me with those big, scared, amber eyes.

Mark sighed. "We're just going to have to pick her up and put her in. If we hang around any longer, we'll miss the train."

I really hated having to force her to do things she was afraid of, but I knew he was right. I gently scooped her up and placed her on her favourite pink and blue blanket next to Kai. "There you go, lovely girl. Snuggle up with your brother. It's going to be OK, I promise."

Mark drove quickly through the early morning traffic, and I could feel myself nodding off, as I hadn't slept much the night before. The journey to Folkestone only took around an hour from our house in Orpington. I woke up with a start as we entered the busy Eurotunnel terminal.

"Come on, sleepy head, we need the passports." Mark laughed as I fumbled around in the glove box, clearly still half asleep.

I eventually handed them to him, and he passed them over to the surly-looking official inside the glass booth. The man looked closely at them, then poked his head out of the open window and peered into the car. I could hear a low growling noise coming from the back seat.

"It's OK, Tammi, calm down." I reached back and tried to stroke her gently. I could see the hackles on the back of her neck standing up. I was really hoping that he wasn't going to come any closer; Tammi was rigid with fear.

"How many dogs do you have?"

"Two," Mark replied.

"That's fine. Here you go, have a good trip." He managed a half smile as he gave the passports back to

Mark, and we proceeded to the French border control. I breathed a big sigh of relief as we were waved straight through.

We followed the road down to the waiting area and parked up in one of the bays. There were huge LED signs everywhere with information about boarding times.

"We've got about 15 minutes before boarding. I'll go and get some coffees. Do you want to take the dogs over there for a wee?" Mark pointed to the fenced-off grass area designated for dogs.

"No, they'll be OK; it'll just stress her out more."

We drank our coffee and then drove down to the familiar platform and onto the waiting train. It was a strange sensation, driving through a train carriage in a car. I was beginning to wonder if we would ever stop when eventually the car in front slowed down, and a fluorescent-clad official signalled for us to park up behind it.

"Handbrake on, into first gear, engine off," he barked as he made his way to the car behind us.

I looked at Tammi anxiously, expecting a reaction; she was crouched down low on the seat, looking petrified. It broke my heart to see her so frightened. At least with the train, we were allowed to stay in the car with the dogs, unlike the ferry, where they would have been left on their own throughout the crossing.

In just under half an hour, we felt the train slowing down. There was a lot of beeping as the huge side exit doors slid open, and we were instructed in both French and English to leave the train in an orderly fashion.

"Don't forget to drive on the other side now."

Mark grinned at me as he navigated past the familiar French road signs, down the slip road and onto the motorway. "You sure you don't want to drive, Ju?"

"Someone needs to keep an eye on the dogs," I said. It was a standing joke between us that I would do anything to get out of driving. Especially on the wrong side of the road. I could never understand how he could drive so far to work and back each day. By the time he got home in the evening, all he could do was eat his dinner and fall asleep. I was looking forward to us spending some quality time together at last. Leah had gone off to Malia with her best friend to work in a bar, and Marcus was in his element, building computer games with his student friends in London.

Mark pulled up at what would be the first of many toll booths on our journey through France. He slowed down to enter the peage and collected the automated ticket from the machine. "Blooming tolls, they cost a small fortune."

I relaxed back into my seat, and my eyes began to droop again. I wasn't really a morning person at the best of times. I was aware of Mark droning on about the French not having to pay road tax and how hard done by we were in the UK.

Another couple of hours had passed before I woke up, just as Mark was pulling into a busy service station.

"I thought the dogs might need a wee. I'm busting." He parked the car and jumped out. "Do you need to go?" he asked as he hopped up and down.

"Not as badly as you! I'll sort the dogs out."

He disappeared round the side of a large brick building, and I turned my attention towards the dogs.

"Right, come on, let's get your leads on."

Kai was happy to be getting out of the car, but Tammi just parked herself behind Mark's seat and refused to budge. I was still trying to coax her out when he returned.

"I'd give those loos a miss if I were you."

I grimaced. "She doesn't want to come out, I think it's too noisy here. You take Kai, and I'll stay here with madam."

Mark took Kai over to the grass verge, where he proceeded to leave his calling card everywhere. He liked to let all the French dogs know the English had arrived! I stayed in the car with a cowering Tammi and wondered whether we would ever be able to do things that normal people did with their dogs. The car park was rammed with cars and caravans, all heading south for the holidays. Mark put Kai back in the car and we set off again. I settled back in my seat, looked out of the window, and soaked up the beautiful, lush greenery of the French countryside. I could feel myself beginning to relax as we sailed past vast fields of bright yellow rape and herds of large brown and white cows. France is huge compared to England, about twice the size, and its population is similar to the UK. I breathed deeply. There was something about the space here that loosened my chest and filled me with a sense of peace. I hoped it would have the same effect on Tammi.

"Let's find a nice place to stop for lunch." Mark smiled. "The French certainly know how to do picnic areas."

After a few miles, I pointed to a familiar sign on the side of the road. "Look, Mark, Aires de repos. That's a picnic site, isn't it?"

A few minutes later, we came off the motorway and parked up next to several wooden picnic tables set in a small pine forest. I inhaled the intoxicating scent and smiled at Mark. "Oh, this is lovely, just what the doctor ordered." I couldn't remember when we last had a picnic, probably when the kids were small.

There were several other families dotted around the designated area, all tucking into lunches of interesting-looking cheeses, little pots of pâtés, and bowls overflowing with mouth-watering tomatoes.

"I'm going to have to visit the ladies, I'm afraid. Why don't you see if madam fancies a picnic? Make sure you keep a tight hold of her; if she gets loose here, we'll never catch her."

When I returned, I was pleased to see both dogs happily sniffing around the base of a huge pine tree.

"How did you get her to come out?"

"I just opened the door, and she shot out! I'm glad I had hold of her lead; she's bloody quick when she wants to be."

I placed my new red gingham tea towel onto the wooden tabletop and unpacked our picnic. I had hastily packed some cheese and crackers the night before, along with a thrown-together salad and some crisps. It was a pitiful offering in such a beautiful setting, but we enjoyed just being here together.

"I think we should celebrate by sharing one of those beers. I'll fetch one from the cool bag."

Mark grinned. "Can you get the dogs' water bowl out, too, please?" We sat there in the warm French sunshine, with the two dogs settled happily beside us. I began to feel the stress of the past few months ebbing away.

"Orpington seems like a million miles away. Look at Tammi. She feels it too. You wouldn't believe it's the same dog; she's so calm here."

"She looks like butter wouldn't melt."

Mark stood up and brushed the crumbs off his T-shirt. "She's doing great, but we need to get going now. Come on, you two, back in the car."

I had to lift Tammi in again, but I noticed that her body wasn't so stiff this time. She settled down onto the back seat quickly, dragging her favourite blanket beneath her haunches.

Five minutes later, we saw the sign for *Pont de Normandie*. My stomach churned at the thought of crossing this huge bridge. I'm terrified of heights. But as the bridge came into view, I couldn't help but admire its beauty. Rising up in front of us like two gigantic white sails, hundreds of intricately connected cable stays enabled the massive structure to span the mouth of the Seine. We joined a queue of slowing traffic as we approached the entrance to the bridge. Then we began the steady climb towards the centre. There was a helpful sign informing us that the highest point was around 215 feet!

"Oh my God! Look at that." I pointed to the tiny boats far below us, on the vast expanse of water. "They look just like toys."

The now familiar peage sign greeted us as we drove off the other end of the bridge. Mark opened the window alongside the glass booth and handed over the correct change.

"Bonjour, Monsieur, merci, bon voyage." The efficient French lady took the money and handed him a small white ticket.

"Merci." I couldn't help laughing as Mark replied in his best French accent. It felt really nice to spend some quality time together at last; I'd almost forgotten how much fun we used to have before life got in the way.

The rest of the journey went quite quickly, and it wasn't long before we entered Brittany. The roads here were much smaller and, at times, quite precarious. Brittany is divided into four departments or regions, and we were heading south towards Morbihan. Vast areas of farmland interspersed with small hamlets of ancient stone buildings flashed past us. It was dusk by the time we arrived at the familiar wooden gates of *la Belle Vilaine*.

9

A Whole New Language

"Bonsoir, Bonsoir." Elaine and Paul rushed over to give us both a hug. They had moved to France from England a few years ago to set up their gite rental and dog training business.

"It's so good to be back; you have no idea." I felt a bit tearful as the stress of the previous few months bubbled to the surface. Finally, we had someone who could help us understand what was going on inside Tammi's head. We had so many questions, but the most pressing one for now was how to get her out of the car and into a strange gite!

Elaine took charge, as usual, in her best schoolteacher voice. "Just leave her in the car and get yourself settled, you two. She's quite safe there with the doors open; she can't get out of the garden."

We entered the little wooden cottage and breathed in the familiar scent, a mixture of furniture polish and lavender. Kai had already made himself at home on one of the comfy armchairs in the lounge. There was a box of goodies and a welcome card strategically placed on the dining room table. Mark picked up a bottle of his favourite beer and waved it under my nose. "They remembered, yay, where's that bottle opener?"

I had a little rummage through the welcome pack while Mark searched through the kitchen drawers. There was the usual selection of biscuits and cakes that looked delicious. "There's a bottle of pear cider in here too, that'll go down nicely with some French cheese and crackers. Oh, it's so nice to be back."

Mark went outside to fetch our luggage and returned with Paul, laden down with cases and bags full of all our holiday essentials. "Oh thanks, Paul, that's so kind of you. Just plonk them down there for now; we can put them away later."

"No, it's OK. We'll put them upstairs, then they're out of the way." All our clothes etc went upstairs into the double bedroom, which overlooked the front garden. There was a lot of creaking from above as the two men climbed the wooden stairs and walked across the upper floor. I was pleased to see the lounge hadn't changed; the old dark wooden furniture gave it a distinguished feel, which blended nicely with some handmade embroidered cushion covers. I threw some of Tammi's blankets onto the sofa. Hopefully, this would help her to feel more at home in these strange surroundings.

There was a knock on the open gite door. It was Elaine armed with a bottle of wine. "No movement from madam yet; she seems quite happy to stay in the car. I've got something that you can try in a bit, guaranteed to get her moving."

She came inside as I retrieved a couple of wine glasses from the kitchen cupboard. Paul and Mark joined us in the lounge, where we chatted for a while. It was great to hear about their three collies and how successful they had been in local agility competitions. Then Elaine turned the conversation towards us. "Now tell us about this new dog of yours; sounds like she's a bit of a handful?"

Mark nodded. "She certainly is. God knows what happened to her over there, but she's terrified of everything. We're just hoping you can work your magic on her while we're here."

"Well, I'll certainly try. You know I like a challenge. Talking of which, shall we see if she's ready to come in yet?" Elaine stood up and walked over to the door. "Right, come on, Paul, let's make ourselves scarce. These two look about ready for bed." As they made their way outside, Elaine handed me something that felt squidgy and smelt awful. "This should do the trick, sheep's lung, dogs love it. See you at eight tomorrow for a dog walk."

"Okay, thanks, goodnight." I stood and watched as they disappeared back inside their adjoining cottage. Holding the offensive article tentatively between my finger and thumb, I made my way over to the car. "Look, Tammi, come and see what Auntie Elaine has given you." She sniffed loudly as I dangled the disgusting stuff just inside the open door. "Come on, you can have some if you get out of the car." I could see Mark looking out at us through the kitchen window. Tammi stood up slowly and stretched out her neck towards my hand, I kept it just out of her reach and backed up towards the gite. Her nose emerged first, still sniffing the air, then very carefully her body followed. Step by agonising step, she crept towards me. "Nearly there, girl, just a few more steps." She stopped at the entrance, as I knew she would. Doorways were still a big issue in Tammi's world, especially strange French ones! I crouched down just inside the door and held out the smelly treat. All at once, she shot through the open door, grabbed the treat, and ran into the lounge.

"Well, look at that, those bloody blankets." Mark shook his head as Tammi carefully settled herself down on the pile I had strategically placed earlier.

The next morning, we were awoken by the unfamiliar sound of a cockerel announcing his presence right across the valley. The gites were surrounded by open fields and ancient woodland. There were a few stone cottages dotted around, but we rarely came across another living soul. It was lovely to just lie in bed and listen to the sounds of the countryside. I wasn't sure what time it was, but thought I'd better get up and let the dogs out. Kai trotted happily out into the small patch of grass that made up the garden. He was finishing his hundredth wee when Tammi crept slowly down from the sofa and joined him outside. She carefully inspected every inch of the garden, then crept back to the safety of her tatty old blankets. We were just finishing our coffee when Elaine appeared at the front window.

"Ready to come for a walk, you two? See you in ten."

With that, she was gone. We looked at each other and laughed. That was so typical Elaine. "I guess we'd better get ready then. Let's hope madam fancies a walk." Mark patted Tammi's head as she looked up expectantly. It wasn't long before we heard barking outside, which signalled that Elaine and Paul and their fur kids were all set to go. Kai was eager to get going too, but I could see Tammi was feeling apprehensive. She ducked down behind the table as soon as I brought her harness out. "Come on, girl, you can do it, don't be scared." I tried to feed her some treats as I quickly clipped on her lead. Mark stepped outside with Kai, and I brought Tammi along behind. Surprisingly, she seemed happy to follow them all through the front gates and down the narrow lane, which ran along the outside of the property. This was the first time we had actually walked her with dogs other than Kai; she seemed to settle down and just go with the flow. The only time she showed any real fear was when a car went past, and then she threw herself down on the ground, shaking until the danger had passed. We followed the road through the village and up into the woods. It was a beautiful morning; the sun shone down on us as we made our way through pine-scented tracks. All the dogs were running around, sniffing each other and investigating all of the fresh smells of the forest. Tammi was no different to the others; it was as if her primal instincts had taken over. She was comfortable in this environment, surrounded by nature; she felt safe. It was such a joy to watch her running around without a care in the world.

The following two weeks just flew by; we learnt so much about how to help Tammi to overcome her fears. It was like learning a whole new language. Instinctively, we had understood that she needed time and patience, but there were so many other things that we hadn't considered until now. We had to change the way she felt about everything; there were no shortcuts. Every time we allowed her to rehearse her fear, it was being reinforced. Rather like having someone suffering from PTSD and forcing them to face their fears daily. By locking someone with a fear of spiders in a room full of them, you are unlikely to cure their fear. *Dogs have a similar ancient FEAR system to us. This can become hyper sensitised if we are frightened badly enough for long enough.* (Panksepp, J. Biven, L. 2012. pg.176) Tammi had probably been scared for most of her life. It was going to be a long, slow process before she could begin to trust anyone.

We spent the whole two weeks working on desensitising and counter-conditioning Tammi to some of the things that scared her. This didn't involve forcing her to face her fears; it was about finding the place where she was comfortable around them. Then changing her perception of the things that she found so terrifying. She really thrived in the vast open spaces of rural Brittany. Although there were still a lot of scary things from her perspective, it was so much quieter than home. When anyone entered our gite, they had been primed to not look at her and to display classic doggie 'calming signals' like sighing and yawning. It was amazing how quickly she would forget her fear and check out their pockets for sausages. This opened up a whole new world to me; I was mesmerised by how well you could communicate with dogs just by reading their body language. I had no idea at this time that my life was going to be forever changed by the things I learnt during these two short weeks in Brittany.

The best thing about being there was being given the time to breathe again. It must be similar to how parents feel when they have a child with special needs. They are on tenterhooks all the time in case their child displays any form of erratic behaviour in public. It's embarrassing when your dog refuses to get into the car and people are watching, or when they jump over a wall into someone's garden and refuse to come out! Here in France, Tammi was allowed to be her crazy little self, and no one batted an eyelid.

Her confidence was improving daily, around other people and their dogs. We tried our hardest never to force her into a situation that made her uncomfortable; however, there were times when we just had to pick her up and carry her into places; it was obvious by her body language that this set her back even further. We tried as much as possible to allow her to decide for herself if she was going to do something. I remember sitting in lots of doorways at this time and just waiting for her to pluck up the courage to come inside. It's quite relaxing once you get over the absurdity of it. I've eaten several meals and drunk numerous glasses of wine, sat on the floor, just waiting for her fear to subside. She reminds me of a slinky toy as she slides commando-style into a room. Once inside, she would settle down beside me, have a good shake-off, and give me that look that said, See, I did it, Mum!

We had some lovely English neighbours in the gite next door, Kate and Fred, who had three dogs of their own and were very experienced at dealing with difficult dogs. They were roped into various role plays with us and Tammi throughout their 'holiday'. Set-ups were carefully managed by Elaine, who gave very specific instructions as to what everyone needed to do. These involved people entering our gite very carefully, maybe wearing a hat or carrying something. Tammi would be somewhere she felt comfortable, usually outside in the garden. The person would sit down quietly in the gite and refrain from giving Tammi eye contact. I would sit with Tammi and reward any calm behaviour with lots of high-value treats. Once she realised the person wasn't a threat, she would move closer and settle down inside again.

There are very few places you can take a fearful animal and find such help and support. We are forever grateful for the skilled help that we received from Elaine and Paul. They introduced us to a whole new world of reward-based training. Since that time, we ourselves have assisted with several other dogs and their rehabilitation while on holiday in Brittany, Thailand, and here in the UK.

Every morning, we set off with the dogs on an amazing walk through the beautiful woods and streams that surrounded the property. We were often joined by Elaine's daughter and her two collies, a neighbour and her little cockapoo, along with Kate and Fred's three; this meant there were around eleven dogs and eight people. All the dogs just got on with each other, and Tammi was able to forget her fears as she blended in with the others. If only we could have stayed there forever.

All too soon, it was time to face the journey back to good old Blighty. It had been a life-changing experience for us; we had learnt so much in such a short time. As we said our tearful goodbyes, we knew that it wouldn't be long before we would return to this piece of 'Doggy Heaven'. It did our hearts the world of good to see Tammi dashing around, looking like a normal dog. We were feeling refreshed and hopeful as we began the long journey home.

10

Living with Tammi

Living with a fearful dog is extremely challenging, and although we loved Tammi to the moon and back, sometimes it was really hard. Visitors were a big problem still, especially Mark's dad, who usually turned up wearing a flat cap and carrying a walking stick. These things were red flags for Tammi, and the sight of him would instantly trigger a fear response. She would bark incessantly until we put her into another room to calm down. There was no reasoning with either of them; at times like this, it was just better to keep her out of the way. For Tammi's sake, we had to learn to be very assertive with people. She wasn't able to speak up for herself, so we became her advocates. People were very well-meaning and generally just wanted to help. However, they didn't have to deal with the fallout, which happened on a regular basis. I began to dread those fateful words, 'It's OK, dogs like me' or 'I'm used to dogs'. You might be brilliant with dogs, but please keep your distance as you're frightening this one!

I remember a particularly irate lady who, against our advice, allowed her spaniel to rush up to Tammi, who was on her lead, and was surprised when she snapped at it. I was subjected to a torrent of abuse as I retrieved her dog and took it back to her.

"That dog's dangerous. It should be wearing a muzzle!" she screamed.

This was a common response from people who allowed their dogs to be out of control around her. I think I would bite, too, if a stranger ran up to me and shoved his nose in my face!

We kitted Tammi out in a harness and high viz tabard for walks, with the instruction, I NEED SPACE, clearly visible on her sides. Unfortunately, however, some people would still try to come up to her and stroke her or allow their dog to get too close to her. We became very adept at scanning the environment when out walking with the dogs, taking evasive action immediately we saw something or someone approaching. Through social media groups, we discovered a whole army of people out there with fearful and reactive dogs. You may not be aware of them, as many will be out very early in the morning or late at night, trying to avoid people and other dogs. The process of desensitisation and counter-conditioning is a long and difficult one. Any number of things can set you back weeks or even months. It's a very slow process where you gradually introduce your dog to the things they are fearful of. Starting at a distance they can cope with, this could be up to a hundred meters or more, in some cases. By pairing the scary thing with something they really love and not allowing them to go over their fear threshold, eventually you can change their emotional response. Tammi was very partial to sausages, cheese, and chicken. Eventually, we were able to move slightly closer to these 'triggers,' the things she found scary, without a reaction. This took a lot of time and patience, but the end result was brilliant. I wish we had kept a diary during this period; it was easy to forget how far she had come in such a short time. Small changes mean so much when you have battled for months and don't seem to be getting anywhere. There were times when she wouldn't even look at her favourite food, she was so stressed. At these moments, unless what we were doing was absolutely vital, like going to the vets or crossing the road, we just stopped and moved her away as quickly as possible. We learnt very quickly to pick our battles carefully. Some days, it was better to just give up and go back home. There was no benefit in forcing her to do something if the fallout would undo months of gradual progress. Living in a busy urban area made it difficult to even leave the house without Tammi freaking out about something. The environment was loaded with triggers, people, dogs, traffic, etc, things that she had to endure every single day.

I became an avid reader of dog training books and followed some great force-free trainers on the internet. It was a difficult process, trying to steer clear of those who thought it was OK to use aversive training methods.

Elaine helped to point us in the right direction. She opened our eyes to so-called celebrity dog trainers, depicted in carefully edited programmes, where the use of force is presented as a positive thing. There are lots of despicable people who make a lot of money out of the suffering they inflict on dogs.

We were determined not to cause any further damage to Tammi, so I made it my mission to educate myself in order to help her rehabilitation. I began to see things through her eyes. She had an early warning system due to her acute hearing and amazing sense of smell. I would be walking calmly down the road with her and Kai, and she would just suddenly stop and refuse to move. Even when there was absolutely nothing around, no traffic, no other people or dogs, she would just freeze or try to run away. It was confusing at first, as there was nothing obvious that could be causing this behaviour. However, within a few moments, someone would appear, or a car would go past; she always knew when something scary was about to happen, it was spooky!

The more I learnt about fearful dogs, the more it became obvious to me that just being in this environment was overwhelming for her. Without realising it, we had been flooding her just by doing what we thought was best. There's a fine line between flooding (forcing an animal to be in a situation, hoping that they will get used to it) and exposing them carefully to things only if they can remain under their fear threshold. She was always so eager to go wherever Kai went that we thought eventually she would take her cue from him and start to relax. However, the reality was that she sometimes found herself in situations that she couldn't cope with; this led to her panicking and shutting down or trying to race for home.

We're all a bit obsessed with thinking that dogs need to be walked every day, but this is not always the best thing for them. I began to discover other forms of enrichment, like laying a trail of chicken for her to follow in the garden. This enabled her to remain nice and relaxed while using her amazing sense of smell to uncover even the tiniest morsel. Activities like this meant she was using mental energy instead of physical energy. We introduced her to some doggy puzzles that we found on the internet. At first, she wouldn't go near them, and we had to persuade Kai to show her what to do. We started by using her favourite foods to get her to move closer to them; eventually, after several days, she would be able to take treats off of them. Some would require the dog to lift up a flap to retrieve treats, and we spent ages lifting things up for her to enable her to find the food. If anything moved too quickly or made a noise, she would be off, in a flash, behind the sofa with her security blanket. Then we would have to wait for her to recover and start again. It was a long, slow process; we often took one step forward and two steps back. I'm not the most patient person, and at times I found it really frustrating, but Tammi never gave up on us. We just knew that she needed us so much; we had to keep going for her sake.

Watching Tammi blossom into a beautiful dog who tried so hard to fit into our confusing world made us very proud. One of her favourite places was the local golf course. If we went there in the evening, we could usually guarantee having the place to ourselves. Kai and Tammi ran amok around the lush, manicured greens and freshly raked bunkers. She would zig-zag between the red and white flags with her 'chase me' face on, and Kai just couldn't resist the challenge. In those moments, Cyprus and KAR seemed a lifetime away; anyone observing us might think we were just a normal family out with our dogs. I just loved watching them playing together; Tammi's coat shone brilliant red, reflecting the warm evening sunshine. Kai loped gracefully after her, his sleek athletic body twisting and turning to keep up with her cunning manoeuvres. Watching the pair of them, so happy and engrossed with each other, made everything worthwhile. If only I could capture these moments and bottle them. I often wondered how much Tammi remembered about her former life. Did she still dream about running around the majestic mountains of Kyrenia with her brother? The thought of her starving and cowering from the sound of the hunters' guns was almost too much to bear. What would have happened to her if we hadn't spotted her hiding in the bush that fateful day?

Would she still be there now, living a semi-feral existence? Or would she have been adopted by someone else? I was often tormented with these thoughts, but I never doubted for a moment that our paths were destined to cross at that precise moment in time.

11

Devastation

It was about a year after we picked up Tammi that we noticed she was slowing down a little. There were some subtle changes in her appearance that started to worry us. She had lost a bit of weight and began shedding more hair than usual. Her nose was very dry, and we had noticed some little scabs on her body. She always had the most beautiful gleaming deep red coat, and lately it had become dull and lifeless. I eventually plucked up the courage to book an appointment with our local vet. I knew this was going to be very stressful for all of us, but we had to find out what was going on.

On the morning of the appointment, Tammi refused to get out of the car; she knew something was up as I had left Kai at home. I went in and told the receptionist that we were just outside and could she let us know when it was our turn to go in. After a few minutes, we were summoned into the surgery. I had to carry Tammi from the car, as it was obvious by her body language that she wanted no part in any of this. As I relayed her list of symptoms to the vet, I became quite emotional. I already knew in my heart what it was, but I just hoped and prayed that I was wrong. They asked me to wait in the waiting room while they took a blood sample from her. Handing her over to the nurse was like a betrayal, but I knew it was for the best. It took about a week for the results to come back. Mark and I couldn't even talk about what might be wrong with her. I knew he quietly feared the worst too. It was a long week. We were dreading that phone call. When it finally came, and the vet confirmed our worst fears, the bottom fell out of our world.

Leishmaniasis is a disease carried by sandflies in hot countries. I had heard about it while in Cyprus; it was common to see dogs suffering from this horrible condition on the streets there. I naively thought that as Tammi had been tested for this disease while in Cyprus, she would be safe. But I was wrong; she must have been bitten by an infected sandfly before leaving the country. Our little girl had carried this like a time bomb inside her for however long, with no visible symptoms until now. The only saving grace was that had it come to light while she was still in Cyprus, she would have been put to sleep straight away. They wouldn't risk her passing it on to the other dogs, however unlikely this is in reality. This disease affects both dogs and humans. She was showing all the classic symptoms, weight loss, dry nose, hair loss, dull, lifeless coat etc. The prognosis is never good, as it affects the internal organs and causes them to eventually fail.

We were numb; this was not part of our plan. Why had God allowed us to come this far, only for us to lose her to this terrible disease? It didn't make any sense, and we just couldn't understand why this was happening. My heart ached day and night; she was such a special dog, my soul mate. I loved her beyond measure, and I was scared that I was going to lose her. She had come so far in such a short time and was finally beginning to enjoy her life here with us and her big brother Kai. She had defied the odds and escaped from a life of misery and fear; this was her time to shine, not die.

After the initial diagnosis, she was put on a course of drugs; these were supposed to alleviate her symptoms, but she quickly began to deteriorate. There was no more chasing Kai around the golf course, as even a short walk around the block left her exhausted. Her beautiful face was covered in the most disgusting scabs, and her hair just fell out by the handful. She was fading away before our very eyes, and we were powerless to help her. When she started drinking excessively and her urine became almost clear, we knew it was a sign that her kidneys were affected. We rushed her back to the vets several times during this period. She was given all sorts of medication, including strong painkillers and drugs for her incontinence, but she seemed to be getting worse.

On one of these visits, the young female vet asked a senior male colleague to have a look at her. As he entered the room and examined Tammi, she hardly acknowledged his presence. I became aware that both of the vets were looking at each other, I knew what they were thinking, but they were wrong.

The older one turned to me. "Mrs Oldfield, I'm so sorry, but we think that it may be time to let her go. You've done everything you can for her; there's nothing else we can do." I was aware of him speaking to me, but I couldn't accept what he was saying. Tammi slowly raised her thin, scabby head, fixed her eyes firmly on me, then closed them and placed her head back on the cold, plastic table. All the fight had gone out of her. My little princess was dying in front of me; she was just skin and bone at this point and so forlorn. Was it fair to keep pushing drugs into her broken little body in the hope that it could buy us a bit more time with her? We had seen miracles happen before, we had come so far, and I didn't want it to end like this. I couldn't speak; I just knew I needed to get her out of there. Tears were pouring down my face as I scooped her up in her special blanket and lifted her gently off the table. I pushed past the two vets, carried my precious baby girl through the busy waiting room, and made my way back to the car.

As I was fumbling around, trying to keep hold of Tammi and get my keys out of my pocket, I became aware of someone behind me. The younger female vet had followed me outside. "You really ought to bring her back inside, Mrs Oldfield. She's very sick."

I avoided looking at her as I placed a lifeless Tammi gently onto the familiar back seat. "She's coming home with me." I heard myself saying these words, but I have no idea why I was saying them. It was as if I had been possessed by something outside of myself. Driving away, I felt strongly that this wasn't the end. I had no idea what we were going to do next, but I knew it didn't involve leaving Tammi behind, not today.

Once again, our friend Elaine came to the rescue. She had been through a dreadful time with one of her dogs, who had been diagnosed with a tumour. She had taken her to a brilliant homeopathic vet with extraordinary results. We had nothing to lose, so we booked an appointment to see Sonia, the vet, who is based in West Sussex, the very next day.

Mark carried Tammi out to the car, wrapped in her holey blanket. She could barely walk now, and we couldn't face any more well-meaning comments from people. She looked so tiny and vulnerable, lying there next to Kai in the back of our car. It suddenly struck me that, terrible as this situation was, at least she had us. The thought of her having to battle this all alone on the streets of Cyprus was unbearable. This is the reality for thousands of stray dogs all over the world. It's heartbreaking to think how they must suffer with no one there to look after them. The lucky ones are picked up by organisations such as KAR and put to sleep.

We finally arrived at the surgery, and Mark went inside to check the coast was clear. Tammi might still react badly to other dogs or people in this strange environment. I picked her up in the blanket and gently placed her feet unsteadily onto the pavement.

"Here, I'll carry her in, shall I?" Mark bent down as if to pick her up.

"NO! Let her walk by herself. She can do it."

We could have just carried her inside, but I wanted them to see how brave she was, not just a bundle in a blanket. Her spirit was still strong, even if her body was failing her. After several minutes of coaxing, we managed to persuade her to go through the door into the surgery. Sonia came out to greet us, and I noticed straightaway how she was very mindful not to give Tammi eye contact, which helped to keep her calm. Tammi crouched low and hid behind Kai as she crept towards the consulting room. We sat down in the comfy armchairs, and after a few minutes she felt comfortable enough to settle down beside us. She looked terrible; the disease had ravaged her beautiful coat; she resembled an old moth-eaten fox fur. We were slightly embarrassed by the state of her; I was still smarting from the comments made by our own vet about putting her to sleep. I couldn't bear it if Sonia thought the same.

"Tell me all about Tammi," she said. "What are her favourite things?" It was nice to be able to tell her about the real Tammi, the beautiful, brave little soul we had fallen in love with. She was interested in knowing all about her and her amazing journey. We were in there for what seemed like hours; no one was in any hurry. It was as far as you could get from our usual vet visits. We were used to being rushed in and out and given a handful of pills before being sent away. We watched both of our dogs settle down and eventually fall asleep on the carpet next to us. The phone didn't ring; no one interrupted us, apart from the receptionist who brought us a lovely cup of tea.

Sonia listened carefully to everything we had to say. I'm sure she could see the devastation in our eyes as we spoke about not wanting to lose our little girl without a fight.

"I can see how much you love Tammi. She's one lucky little dog to have found you both. I really wish I had a cure for her condition, but I don't. As you know, she is very sick, and her prognosis is not good, but there are things we can try in order to slow down the process." She gave us something that no one else had up to this point; she gave us hope. It's just a small four-letter word, but it meant so much to us at the time. No one made any promises about a cure; we knew there wasn't one. We just wanted a bit more time with our beloved girl. Both dogs slept soundly all the way home; it was as if Sonia had put a spell on them. Mark and I also felt strangely calm for the first time in weeks. That evening, we fed the dogs and added some of the remedies that Sonia had given us to put in Tammi's food. She was also due one of the strong painkillers at this time, and I felt a little apprehensive as I moved the box away from her bowl. She ate everything quickly, which was unusual. Lately, she had become a bit picky with her food; I was probably imagining it. I didn't want to get my hopes up, only to have them crushed again.

Over the next few weeks, life went on around us pretty much as normal; we were like figures trapped inside a snow globe. Aware of the hustle and bustle of life on the outside but trapped inside. We were consumed by our daily crusade to save our beautiful princess. It seemed like an impossible task; she was a shadow of her former self. Lacking in energy, she slept for hours on end. Sometimes she scared me, and I had to poke her to ensure she was still with us. Mealtimes were spent sitting on the kitchen floor, trying to encourage her to eat. I cooked all of her favourite foods, sausages, chicken, and liver. Kai was always on hand to help out if she couldn't manage anything. She would slowly lick tiny morsels of food from my hand as I sat there praying, just willing her to eat one more handful.

Gradually, as the weeks passed, she began to improve. At first, I didn't believe it. She began to eat properly, and her coat started to grow back. We were really cautious as we couldn't face another setback. She wanted to go on walks again and got excited when we got her lead out. It was amazing! There she was on death's door only weeks ago. Now, we could see that she was beginning to get back to her old self. It really was a miracle. Every day she got stronger, the scabs came off, and her fur grew back. We began to see her beautiful burnished red coat emerging again. I just couldn't believe it; our prayers had been answered.

It was fantastic to have our cheeky, blanket-stealing little monkey back again. At first, we kept looking for signs of that terrible disease. But eventually, as the weeks turned into months and she was still running around chasing Kai, we accepted that, for now, she was back. We could breathe again, and life returned to normal. As we watched the dogs playing together that spring, we knew we were on borrowed time. She was so happy running around the golf course without a care in the world. It made me smile and weep at the same time. I wanted her to live forever.

Every moment with her was precious, and I made sure we cherished this special time. Everything else went on hold; she was the centre of our world. I would spend hours sitting on the hard kitchen floor, gently brushing her and telling her how beautiful she was. There were still lots of things that scared her: cars, doorways, headlights, pushchairs etc. Desensitisation is a slow process, especially with a dog who is already overwhelmed with everyday things in general. I read so many books about dog training at this time, and I began to understand the importance of taking things slowly. Debbie Jacobs' book, *A Guide to Living With & Training a Fearful Dog,* was especially helpful to me, as it changed my expectations for Tammi.

I began to see who she really was, not who I wanted her to be. I could advocate for her, but SHE decided when things were safe, not me. It was so difficult to understand what was going on in her head. I could read her body language quite well now, those minute signals that told me she was about to freak out. I knew all the things to look out for on a walk and when it was safer to just cross the road. But I still got it wrong. Sometimes, I would come back in tears because Tammi had spotted something scary before I did. Suddenly, she would hurl herself into a bush, too terrified to move. We were making progress slowly; my poor, broken little dog was trying so hard to survive in this alien environment.

Spring turned into summer, and we spent many hours just exploring different places with the dogs. Long woodland walks in the sunshine were her favourite, especially when we managed to avoid meeting other people. There are lots of beautiful places to visit around the Kent countryside, so long as you avoid going at weekends or bank holidays!

I was only working part-time for the police now, which gave me a lot more time to spend with the dogs. I kept in regular contact with Elaine and Sonia, giving them progress reports. They were as amazed as we were at how well she was doing.

12

The Return

"Are you OK?" Mark reached for my hand across the sticky pub table.

I took a deep, shuddery breath and tucked my soggy tissue up the sleeve of my old grey cardigan. "Yeah, I think so." I felt strangely relieved, if I was being honest. I'd been dreading this day for so long.

Watching my darling Tammi slowly deteriorate over the past few weeks had been almost too much to bear. Seeing the signs of Leish ravishing her beautiful coat again had hit me like a juggernaut. I wanted to scream, 'NO! NO! Please, not again'. She was just beginning to enjoy her life here with us.

This time, the symptoms came thick and fast; her weight plummeted until she looked like a skeleton. Her hip bones stuck out at an alarming angle, and we could count all of her ribs. The sight of her clear, watery urine was a sure sign that her damaged kidneys were failing. She became very lethargic and slept endlessly throughout those last days. Sometimes, I was afraid to touch her as I couldn't make out if she was still breathing.

"We did the right thing, you know."

I tried to smile, but tears just rolled down my cheeks. Mark was struggling to know what to say to me; I think we were both in shock. So much had happened in such a short time it was difficult to process it all.

"We couldn't let her go on like that any longer." Mark took a long sip of beer and placed the pint glass down onto the table.

That morning had started like many others. Mark had gone off to work, and I'd got up a bit later and spent some time watching TV with the dogs. Tammi hadn't eaten her breakfast again, so I'd tried to coax her with some chicken, but she wasn't interested.

She settled herself down on the armchair and slept. Kai was eager to go for a walk, so I dressed quickly and got his lead out of the cupboard. Tammi normally gave a little wag of her tail at this point; today, she didn't move. I kissed the top of her bony head. "We won't be long, darling." I felt a bit uneasy leaving her alone like that, but Kai was desperate to go out. I opened the front door, and he bounded out into the sunshine. I held on tightly to his lead as we turned right out of the little wooden gate that formed a barrier between our front garden and the busy road outside.

We did a short walk around the block just so that Kai could cock his leg on every lamppost. The semi-detached houses were all very similar to ours; most had concrete driveways with several cars parked on them. As we stopped for the zillionth time, I looked around at some of the remaining gardens. May was such a lovely month. I watched, mesmerised, as a chunky bee defied gravity and carefully visited each gently swaying yellow daffodil head. The pungent scent of roses filled my nostrils, velvet petals of pink, yellow, orange and red. I love springtime; everything is bursting into life after the winter sleep. Suddenly, I was jerked out of my daydream as Kai insisted on moving to another lamppost.

In no time at all, we were back outside our familiar old, wooden front door. I carefully put my key into the lock and turned it, pushing the door open gently; I didn't want to disturb Tammi. I unclipped Kai's lead, and he bounded up the hallway straight into the lounge. I followed quickly and noticed he had stopped right beside her; he was giving her a thorough sniffing. I hesitated for a moment; her ravaged little body was remarkably still. Kai nudged her with his long-pointed nose, and I was relieved to see her head come up.

Slowly, she turned towards me with those beautiful amber eyes, once shining and happy, now full of pain.

I stroked her head gently, carefully avoiding the disgusting clusters of scabs. "It's alright, baby girl. I know, you've had enough." I don't understand how she told me, but I knew straightaway. I could barely speak on the phone to Mark. "It's time. You need to come home, now."

I had been dreading this moment ever since the Leish came back, but now we had to do what was right for

Tammi. Sonia understood straightaway and just said bring her in when you're ready. I snuggled up in the armchair next to her broken little body and told her how beautiful she was and how much we all loved her. Kai kept poking her with his nose, willing her to wake up. I think he knew she was close to the end.

Mark came slowly into the lounge, still wearing his work overalls and crouched down beside our little tableau. "Are you ready to go?"

I didn't dare speak as I knew I would have changed my mind. I looked up at Mark and nodded. "Okay. What about Kai? Shall we take him with us?"

I shook my head. "I think we should leave him here; I can't bear the thought of him being there at the end."

"He might wonder where she is when we come back?"

"I know," I sobbed. "I just can't, I'm sorry, can we just go?"

The journey to the vets took about an hour; thankfully, there wasn't much traffic around as it was coming up to midday. I sat in the back with Tammi, who was wrapped in what was left of her favourite pink blanket. She slept soundly, draped across my lap, blissfully unaware of what was coming. Sunlight streamed in through the car windows, bathing us all in a golden glow. Inside, my heart was breaking. I didn't want to let her go, not now, not ever. Through my tears, I watched cars speeding by, full of people with busy lives. I never wanted this journey to end.

So much had happened since that first glimpse of those beautiful amber eyes, capturing my heart in a faraway land. We had seen things we never thought possible. Saving Tammi had changed our lives in so many ways. No longer accepting things at face value; if someone said it couldn't be done, we looked for another way. There was a third dimension to life, an invisible power that carried us when we reached the end of ourselves. This didn't mean that our prayers were always answered; sometimes we just accepted the answer was no. I had become obsessed with learning all about dog behaviour; I instinctively knew my future would involve helping other dogs like Tammi.

We arrived outside the familiar whitewashed surgery far too soon. Mark opened the back door and gently lifted Tammi's emaciated body from my lap. It took all my strength to stop myself from screaming as I carefully wrapped the familiar blanket around her. I didn't want her to go. I followed them into the empty waiting room, where cheerful cushions adorned the comfy chairs. Pictures of happy, smiling dogs surrounded us. It was more than I could bear.

The receptionist recognised us straight away. "Mr and Mrs Oldfield, please come through, Sonia is waiting for you in her office." As we walked past, she glanced at the little bundle Mark was carrying and gave us a sympathetic smile.

Sonia looked up as we entered her office. It was a lovely, homely room with sofas and carpets designed to make clients and animals feel comfortable. I had never seen anyone in a white coat at the surgery; everyone wore casual clothes. Homeopathic vets do the same training as other vets and then do additional qualifications in homeopathy. It's a whole different level of service, where clients are treated as individuals and treatments are based on the principle that like cures like. No stone is left unturned when it comes to helping a patient, especially when conventional medicine doesn't work.

Sonia waved us towards the sofa. I couldn't speak; tears were rolling down my cheeks and dripping off my chin. She lifted up the blanket and used her stethoscope to listen to Tammi's heart. I couldn't look at her. I didn't want to hear what I knew she was going to say. I just focussed on stroking my beautiful girl as she slept in her daddy's arms. Sonia sat down and looked straight at us. "You've done the right thing bringing her in today. No one could have done more for her than you have. Now, it's time for you to let her go. Take as much time as you need. When you're ready, let me know, and I'll give her a sedative." Then she left us alone with our beautiful baby girl.

There was a comfy-looking dog bed on the floor, surrounded by blankets. Mark gently placed Tammi on the bed and covered her protruding ribcage with her special pink blanket. We laid down beside her and cuddled her small, still body between us. I wanted to be strong as I knew she would still be aware of my emotional state. We had become so close over the past few months; I could feel her pain, and I'm sure she was aware of mine too. I placed my lips close to her small, fuzzy, pointed ears and whispered softly to her, "I love you, baby girl. Be brave and fly away now. We'll find you again, I promise, then we'll be together forever." She looked really peaceful lying there, no longer afraid. I had imagined this moment so many times, and now it was actually happening, I felt strangely detached, as if I wasn't really there. Just watching from a distance.

All this time, I'd been fighting to keep her alive. How could I let her go? I thought about the first time I had set eyes on her, hiding under the bush; she was so scared. How we spent hours trying to get her to come out and finally eat the hotel sausages. I remembered the euphoria when the law changed and it became possible for us to adopt her; that dreadful journey across Europe when she had to endure 12 days in the couriers' van, bringing her home for the first time, and realising our work was just beginning. All these memories were flooding my mind, like an old cine film going round and round. I would give anything to go back to the beginning and do it all again.

"Shall we get Sonia to come back in?" Mark's voice startled me. I knew he was trying to be strong, but I could hear the shake in his voice.

I couldn't take my eyes off Tammi. I wanted to hold onto every last second.

Sonia came in and knelt down beside us. "I'm going to give her an injection, and she's going to fall asleep quite quickly; she won't feel anything after that. I'll leave you to say goodbye, and only when you're ready will I come back. Take your time; there's no rush."

We both nodded, and Mark held my hand.

As Sonia gave her the injection, Tammi looked up at us and then slowly closed her eyes forever. We both bent down and kissed her goodbye as she went to sleep. She looked so small lying there, her lovely coat ruined, her beautiful face full of scars. I knew deep in my heart that her short life had changed me forever. She had lit a fire inside of me, a hunger to learn how to help other dogs like her. I could no longer turn a blind eye to the cruelty and suffering of dogs around the world. Tammi was my heart dog, my soul mate. Now I had to continue my journey without her.

13

Tammi's Legacy

As I open the front door, the howling gets louder. I am instantly mobbed by three furry bundles, eager to get outside. "OK, come on, you lot, sit down and let me put your harnesses on, quiet now." They eventually calm down and let me attach their leads. We have five rescue dogs now; three of them have come from six thousand miles away in Thailand. Throughout the last seven years, Mark and I have spent a lot of time as volunteers for the Soi Dog Foundation. Our daughter Leah introduced us to this amazing place when she came across it during a gap year spent travelling around Asia with her boyfriend, James. We now choose to spend most of our holidays walking hundreds of rescue dogs on the beautiful island of Phuket.

It's just a short walk to the field at the end of our lane, more of a driveway really, accessed through a pair of ancient stone pillars. "Morning, George." I wave as I scoot past our lovely, elderly neighbour, pottering around his allotment as usual. Everyone knows everyone around here, something that takes a lot of getting used to. We've been living on the southern tip of Cornwall for about five years now, and I'm still blown away by these beautiful surroundings, especially on days like this. Orpington seems a million miles away. I don't miss the noise and the traffic one bit.

I unclip the dogs' leads, and they race to get over the smooth, stone stile, then charge, full pelt, across the tree-lined field. As I carefully pick my way over the slippery Cornish death trap, three panting, excited dogs come racing back towards me.

We take our usual route around the edge of George's field, lined with apple trees covered in beautiful white blossom. The air is filled with birdsong as busy parents rush to and fro with morsels of food for their little ones. I love this time of year; spring always fills me with hope, and there's new life springing up everywhere. I often think about Tammi on my walks and how much she would have enjoyed it here. The vast open spaces and quiet country lanes would have suited her down to the ground.

Losing Tammi was incredibly hard for all of us; she was such a big part of our lives, and her passing left a huge gap. Everything seemed so pointless without her. Kai was missing her too; he slept more than he used to and would sit up and look hopeful whenever someone opened the front door. It was heartbreaking to see the disappointment in his eyes as he realised it wasn't her. We went on lots of long, tearful walks together around the Kent countryside. I kept asking the same question over and over again: Why had we come so far with Tammi only to lose her so soon? It just didn't make sense to me. Finding and rescuing Tammi had been a real roller coaster ride, which had left me feeling bereft. I was determined that her short life would have a purpose; I didn't believe that she had come into our lives by accident. She had left me with a hunger to help other dogs like her; I just needed to find the right path.

My friend Elaine had done her training with the Institute of Modern Dog Trainers, so I thought this was a good place to start. The methods they use are all science-based, which means they have been proven to work. I agree wholeheartedly with their reward-based methods, which prohibit the use of force in training. In 2015, I attended the initial two-day course in Essex, facilitated by Steve Mann, who is the founder of this amazing organisation. After a lot of home study and several other courses, I eventually qualified as a dog behaviourist. It felt great having passed the assessment, but I knew I still had a long way to go. Dog behaviour is a fascinating and complex subject, and eight years later, I am still learning new things. No two dogs are the same. Just like us, they have their own individual personalities, shaped by good or bad experiences.

We make our way along the overgrown footpath, past the enduring 14th-century Grade Church. The early morning sun climbs high up above the ancient rooftop, sorely in need of restoration. Crumbling gravestones lean precariously, like drunken sailors, battered by centuries of Cornish storms. Many of their occupants are now nameless as they continue their eternal rest.

"Kai, Roo, Lottie, come here." I clip the dog's leads on as we approach the wooden gate that opens onto a narrow lane. We don't get too many cars down this way, but you never know when one might appear. Summertime brings a lot of visitors to Cornwall, and not everyone drives slowly round the winding lanes. I feel very lucky to be living in such a beautiful part of the country, running my own dog behaviour business. I see all types of dogs, ranging from puppies to older dogs, with a variety of behaviour problems. I still get goosebumps when someone rings me and describes a rescue dog that is completely shut down. I feel like I have a superpower when it comes to fearful dogs, I understand how they are feeling, and I'm able to communicate with them in a way that I can't really explain. It's like I can see their struggle; they want to trust people, but past experience has made them wary. It takes a lot of time and patience to build trust with a fearful dog, but there is no better feeling than the moment you know you have reached them. Tammi left me with this gift, and I am eternally grateful to her. Dogs are my life now; they are the reason I get up each day. I can't imagine doing anything else.

Sadly, our move to Cornwall came too late for Tammi, but I still feel she's here, in spirit, with me. Going to Cyprus and finding her hiding in the bush that day was no accident. I believe we were destined to be there at that precise time. We had no way of knowing that the decision we made to bring her home was going to change the course of our lives. Tammi taught me more about dog behaviour in those two short years than any training course or book has ever managed to do. There's no substitute for actual hands-on experience with animals; each one is unique. I feel privileged to have had such an excellent teacher.

Sleep tight, my little angel.

Kai and Tammi posing in the conservatory

THE BLANKET THIEF

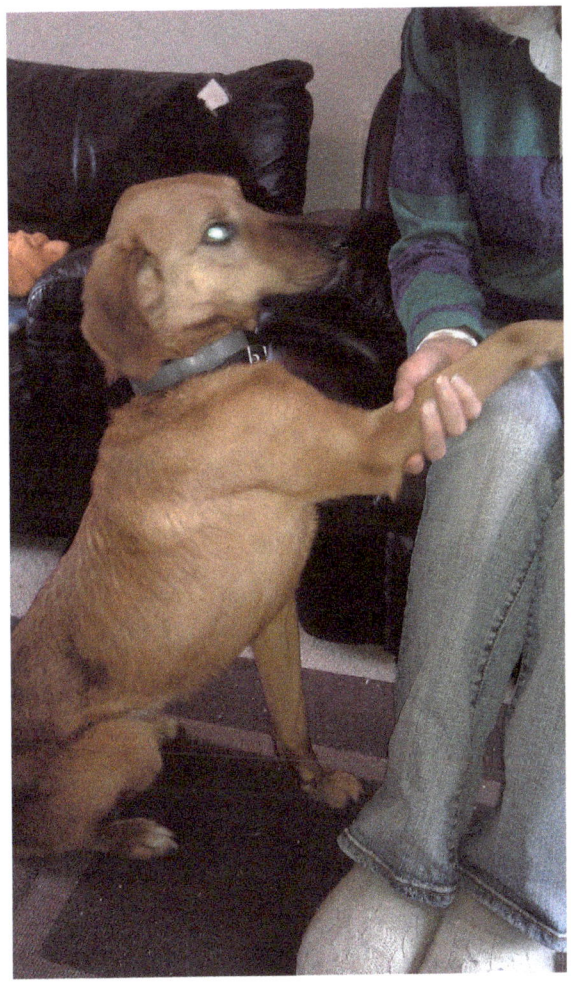

Tammi and me holding hands

Tammi and Mark

THE BLANKET THIEF

Checking out the beach

Tammi having a little snooze

THE BLANKET THIEF

At La belle Vilaine

Kai and Tammi besties

Tammi wearing the Help for Heroes collar

Tammi with Yuliyan

Sally Grist

Acknowledgements

There are so many people I need to thank, first and foremost my husband Mark, my fellow traveller, thank you for your constant encouragement and your ability to always look on the bright side. This book would still be held hostage by the computer without your constant patience and negotiation skills. To my children Marcus and Leah, for being such great kids, despite having to put up with my crazy schemes, I'm so proud of the amazing adults you have become. To all the wonderful people at Kyrenia Animal Rescue, past and present, who made everything possible, especially Suzan Femi and Yuliyan, thank you for rescuing Tammi and all the other poor discarded souls. To the amazing Animal Couriers, for taking such good care of all the dogs on that epic journey. To Kath Morgan, fellow author and teacher, and all the members of our online writing group, thank you for your skill and encouragement, which enabled me to bring my story to life. Thanks to Mary Keely and Brian Jenkins and all the members of the Ruan Minor Reading group, for your constant encouragement. Special thanks to Angela Agutter for reading aloud my early draft and giving me the courage to continue. To Paul and Elaine Clark from La Belle Vilaine Gites, for your kindness and encouragement, you taught us so much, thank you. Also, to Kate and Fred who helped with Tammi's rehabilitation in Brittany. My heartfelt thanks to Sonia, and everyone at The Holistic Veterinary Medicine Centre, for being such wonderful, caring people. Thank you for giving us some more time with our precious baby girl. To Steve Mann for creating the amazing IMDT, which has helped to revolutionise dog training. Thank you for all the brilliant Trainers and courses, that have given me a whole new career. To fellow authors, Elaine Singer and Eve Collet- Martin, thank you for your encouragement and amazing reviews. To Alison and Andrew Damant for proof reading and friendship. Not forgetting, Julie Scott and everyone at Grosvenor House Publishing, thank you for working tirelessly, to bring my inane ramblings to life!

Thank you for buying my book. If you would like to know more about KAR or make a donation to this amazing place, please go to http://www.kartrnc.org

For Dog training and behaviour advice please go to my website https://www.cadgwithcanines.co.uk/

For information about the IMDT please go to http://www.imdt.uk.com

In memory of Tammi and Kai two beautiful souls, together again in heaven.

Bibliography

Panksepp, J. Biven, L. **The Archaeology of Mind. Neuroevolutionary Origins of Human Emotions.** W. W. Norton & Company, 2012.

Jacobs, D. **A Guide to Living with and Training a Fearful Dog.** Corner Dog Press, 2008.

Rugaas, T. **On Talking Terms with Dogs: Calming Signals.** Dogwise Publishing, 2006.

www.ingramcontent.com/pod-product-compliance
Lightning Source LLC
Chambersburg PA
CBHW041927090426
42743CB00021B/3466